Ministering to Persons with Mental Retardation and Their Families

Gene Nabi

Convention Press/Nashville, Tennessee

Dedicated to
Joy
David
Cheryl
Scott
Kenneth
Steven

This book is the text for a course in the
subject area Age Division and Special Group Characteristics of
the Church Study Course.

Dewey Decimal Classification Number: 259.4
Subject Headings
CHURCH WORK WITH THE MENTALLY HANDICAPPED //
Mentally Handicapped
MINISTRY TO FAMILIES
Printed in the United States of America

About the Author

Gene Nabi is consultant, Special Ministries Unit, Bible Teaching Division of The Sunday School Board of the Southern Baptist Convention, Nashville, Tennessee. Born in Jacksonville, Florida, he holds a Bachelor of Arts degree with a major in English from Florida State University, Tallahassee.

His experience in the field of mental retardation started with his son Scott, born in 1961. Mr. Nabi actively served as a volunteer leader in several organizations, including the School for Handicapped Children (Virginia); Nashville Institute for Neurological Development, Inc.; Tennessee Foster Grandparents, Inc.; and Tennessee Special Olympics, Inc.

He served as Executive Director of the Tennessee Association for Retarded Citizens and President of Mental Retardation Services.

His articles on mental retardation have appeared in various publications.

He has conducted conferences throughout the Southern Baptist Convention and at conference centers at Glorieta, New Mexico, and Ridgecrest, North Carolina.

He is active in developing interdenominational cooperation and fellowship in the area of mental retardation.

He and his wife, Joy (a registered nurse), are the parents of four sons and a daughter.

Foreword

The Bible has painted for us many pictures of God. Christians know Him as Creator, Sustainer, and Redeemer. Perhaps the most intimate picture of God is Father. Involved in this description of God are love, grace, peace, compassion, mercy, and, yes, accountability and judgment.

One concept describes God, and it runs like a golden thread through every picture in the Bible. That concept is outreach—to every person in every place, regardless of circumstance—outreach, the heartthrob of God.

The burden of this book is to challenge Southern Baptist churches to reach and to minister to handicapped persons and, in particular, to persons with mental retardation and their families.

Christ was, and is, the role model for each believer. Surely this is evident in the New Testament as He ministered to the needs of handicapped persons.

My prayer for you, the reader, is that our heavenly Father would open your eyes to see these persons who need to see and feel your reaching and ministering love.

D. *Lewis White, Supervisor*
CPS *Special Ministries Unit*
Bible Teaching Division

Introduction

The problem of mental retardation has gained considerable attention over the past twenty-five years.

First, a President, influenced by his retarded sister, brought governmental action—and funds—to focus on the problem. Encouraged by this, private voluntary groups moved to establish equity for retarded persons: mandatory education, availability of health and preventive measures, and various other rights that are given without question to all other persons.

Second, many Southern Baptists served as volunteer workers and leaders within this movement and continually built a strong case for the need for an organized church ministry to retarded persons. The Sunday School Board of the Southern Baptist Convention responded by including mentally retarded persons within the scope of its special ministries. Further, it encouraged state conventions and local churches to start and develop mental retardation ministries.

Third, in 1983 The Sunday School Board began increasing its emphasis on ministering, emphasizing a ministry to the families of retarded persons and recognizing that the church could reach families through some basic, simple, practical approaches.

This book is a result of this increased emphasis. It is not a book on how to teach. It is not meant to be comprehensive or complete. Rather, it is meant to suggest ways that the church can minister to mentally retarded persons and their families.

Responding to the needs of handicapped persons and their families was an extremely high priority in the earthly ministry of Jesus.

It is a priority we have no business changing.

*All photographs are by Gene Nabi
unless otherwise indicated.
Cover design and illustrations are
by Dean Shelton.*

Contents

About the Author 5
Foreword 6
Introduction 7
Chapter 1   **An Old Problem Made New** 11
    The New Challenge 11
    Conditions Were Deplorable 12
    What Is Mental Retardation? 14
    What Causes Mental Retardation? 14
    Many Levels of Retardation 15
    Classification and Characteristics 17
    Differences Between Mental Retardation and Mental
       Illness 18
    Mental Retardation Is Not Hopeless 19
    The Sunday School Board Responds 20
    Attitudes Are Reflected in Terms 21
    Ethical Issues 21
    Bill of Rights 24
Chapter 2   **Why Have a Ministry?** 27
    Jesus Set the Example 27
    The Urgent Task 27
    Our Spiritual Weaknesses Mirrored 29
    With Ministry, Improvement 29
    Reminder of Priorities 31
    Allows Family Ministry 31
    Positive Side Effects 32
    Do Unto Others 32
Chapter 3   **Starting a Ministry for Mentally Retarded Persons** .. 35
    Make a Commitment 35
    Pray for Direction 36
    Seek Biblical Insight 37
    Educate Yourself 37
    Educate the Pastor 40
    Educate the Congregation 43
    Recruit and Train Teachers 46
    Develop an Outreach Program 47
    Prepare Curriculum 47
    Prepare the Room 47
    Set a Date and Start! 48
Chapter 4   **Outreach** 51
    Reasons for Not Developing an Outreach Ministry ... 51
    Seven Outreach Methods 52

Visitation Is Personal, Powerful 57
Chapter 5 Recruiting and Training Teachers 59
Who Makes a Good Teacher? 59
Where Can Good Teachers Be Found? 63
Should Parents Teach? 63
Who Does Not Make a Good Teacher? 63
Prepare the Prospective Teacher 64
After Enlistment, Train 64
Chapter 6 Ministering to the Family 67
Mental Retardation Has a Powerful Influence 67
Wide Range of Family Attitudes 68
Classical Reactions of Family 70
How Can the Church Minister? 72
The High Cost of a Personal Ministry 73
Some Personal Ways to Minister 74
Theological Issues of Mental Retardation 74
Problems of Parents 76
How the Church Can Minister in Tangible Ways 80
Chapter 7 Curriculum 83
Curriculum Defined 83
What and How Do I Teach? 83
Teachers Are Learners 84
Available Resources 86
Good Teaching Requires Planning 90
The Key Is to Adapt 92
Special Problems 93
Chapter 8 Mental Retardation and Conversion 99
Two Points of View 99
Crystal Clear Clarification 101
Lost, Saved, Safe 101
How to Minister 104
Myths and Facts 105
Chapter 9 New Hope 107
What Message from the Church? 107
What Message from the Bible? 108
Is There Hope in Prevention and Treatment? 109
Is There Hope for a Cure? 109
Chapter 10 Finally 113
Appendix A: Organizations and Agencies As Resources 116
Appendix B: State Convention Resources 118
Appendix C: References Recommended for the Church Media
Library 121
Appendix D: Sunday School Leadership Diplomas in Special
Ministries—Mentally Retarded 122
Appendix E: The Church Study Course 123

This is the way it was in 1912:
The social and economic burdens of uncomplicated feeblemindedness are only too well known. The feebleminded are a parasitic, predatory class, never capable of self-support or of managing their own affairs.
The great majority ultimately become public charges in some form.
They cause unutterable sorrow at home and are a menace and danger to the community. . . . Every feebleminded person, especially the highgrade imbecile, is a potential criminal.[1]

---

[1]W. E. Fernald, "The Burden of Feeblemindedness," *J. of Psychoasthenics,* XVIII, 1912, pp. 90-98.

Chapter 1

An Old Problem Made New

The New Challenge

Beginning in the early 1960s, the problem of mental retardation was suddenly brought to the attention of the American people in a new way. The newly elected President, John F. Kennedy (who had a mentally retarded sister), created a special panel of outstanding persons in the field of mental retardation. Its task was to recommend a plan of action for responding to the problem that affects about 3 percent of the American population, or about 6½-7 million persons.

Table 1 shows the estimated population of mentally retarded persons by state. A similar estimate can be made for counties, cities, or towns by computing 3 percent of their populations.

However, this estimate includes only retarded persons, not the family members who also are affected and influenced—both good and bad ways—by the presence of a retarded person. Assuming that each retarded person has an average of four immediate family members, one can estimate the number of family members directly affected by mental retardation by multiplying the number of mentally retarded persons by 4. For example, an estimate of the number of family members affected by mental retardation in the United States is 6½ million times 4, or 26 million people.

Most of these persons are not active church members, often because of the problem of mental retardation. But these persons need the ministry of the church and the gospel message.

Conditions Were Deplorable

Prior to the 1960s when the need for radical improvements in the care, teaching, and training of mentally retarded persons began to receive much greater public and governmental attention, most existing services and institutions were deplorable.

- Institutions were called human warehouses.
- The rights of mentally retarded persons were ignored and abused.
- Special education programs in the public school system were not mandatory.
- State governments assigned responsibility for mental retardation programs to the department of corrections.
- Retarded persons were labeled "criminally insane," "feebleminded," "idiots," "imbeciles," "morons," and other negative terms.

TABLE 1

1980 STATE POPULATIONS
with 3 percent estimate of mentally retarded persons

STATE	1980 POPULATION	3% Estimate
ALABAMA	3,890,061	116,702
ALASKA	400,481	12,014
ARIZONA	2,717,866	81,536
ARKANSAS	2,285,513	68,565
CALIFORNIA	23,668,562	710,056
COLORADO	2,888,834	86,665
CONNECTICUT	3,107,576	93,227
DELAWARE	595,225	17,857
D.C.	637,651	19,130
FLORIDA	9,739,992	292,200

STATE	1980 POPULATION	3% Estimate
GEORGIA	5,464,265	163,928
HAWAII	965,000	28,950
IDAHO	943,935	28,318
ILLINOIS	11,418,461	342,554
INDIANA	5,490,179	164,705
IOWA	2,913,387	87,402
KANSAS	2,363,208	70,896
KENTUCKY	3,661,433	109,843
LOUISIANA	4,203,972	126,119
MAINE	1,124,660	33,740
MARYLAND	4,216,446	126,493
MASSACHUSETTS	5,737,037	172,111
MICHIGAN	9,258,344	277,750
MINNESOTA	4,077,148	122,314
MISSISSIPPI	2,520,638	75,619
MISSOURI	4,917,444	147,523
MONTANA	786,690	23,601
NEBRASKA	1,570,006	47,100
NEVADA	799,184	23,976
NEW HAMPSHIRE	920,610	27,618
NEW JERSEY	7,364,158	220,925
NEW MEXICO	1,299,968	39,999
NEW YORK	17,557,288	526,719
NORTH CAROLINA	5,874,429	176,233
NORTH DAKOTA	652,695	19,581
OHIO	10,797,419	323,923
OKLAHOMA	3,025,266	90,758
OREGON	2,632,663	78,980
PENNSYLVANIA	11,866,728	356,002
RHODE ISLAND	947,154	28,415
SOUTH CAROLINA	3,119,208	93,576
SOUTH DAKOTA	690,178	20,705
TENNESSEE	4,590,750	137,723
TEXAS	14,228,383	426,852
UTAH	1,461,037	43,831
VERMONT	511,456	15,344
VIRGINIA	5,346,279	160,388
WASHINGTON	4,130,163	123,905
WEST VIRGINIA	1,949,644	58,489
WISCONSIN	4,705,335	141,161
WYOMING	470,816	14,125
TOTAL U.S.	226,504,825	6,795,145

13

What Is Mental Retardation?

There are many misconceptions about mental retardation. Difficult to define, the term is considered a negative label. It is often mistaken for mental illness. As defined by the American Association on Mental Deficiency:

"Mental retardation refers to significantly subaverage general intellectual functioning existing concurrently with deficits in adaptive behavior and manifested during the developmental period." [1]

In this definition:

- *Intellectual functioning* generally refers to one's ability to learn, to reason or make good judgment, to understand or comprehend meaning, to deal with new situations, to solve problems, and to retain information or to remember.
- *Adaptive behavior* refers to such functions as social skills, communication, self-direction, self-help skills, and antisocial or unusual behavior.
- *Developmental period* is the period of time between conception and the eighteenth birthday.

There has been disagreement among professional workers about a precise definition, but there is general agreement that *mental retardation refers to persons whose intellectual and social development is much lower than most other persons of the same age.*

Mental retardation is a *condition.* Persons with mental retardation exhibit the condition through various characteristics. For example, inability to communicate, poor self-help skills, poor judgment, poor memory, and poor social skills are representative characteristics. The presence of these characteristics does not necessarily indicate mental retardation.

What Causes Mental Retardation?

There are 250-350 causes of mental retardation. These can be generally grouped into the following categories:

---

[1] From *Classification in Mental Retardation* (Washington, D.C.: American Association on Mental Deficiency), p. 11.

- Genetic
- Hereditary
- Prenatal
- During delivery
- Immediately after delivery
- Postnatal
- During the early childhood developmental years

Specific causes of mental retardation cannot be pinpointed in about 75 percent of all retarded individuals.

Most of the mild forms of mental retardation have no apparent physical cause and may be due to adverse environmental conditions experienced in early childhood. According to the American Association on Mental Deficiency, about 89 percent of all mentally retarded individuals are mildly retarded. No organic cause of their condition has been identified. For practically all of the individuals in this category, there is no identifiable organic cause of their condition. The prevalence of mild mental retardation is 13 times greater among the poor than among those in middle- and upper-level groups.

Children born and raised in urban ghettos or impoverished rural areas are more likely to be diagnosed as mentally retarded than are children from middle-class suburban neighborhoods. From 85 to 90 percent of those who are mildly retarded with no identifiable organic or physical cause were disadvantaged by environmental conditions such as poverty, racial and ethnic discrimination, and family distress. About 1.5% of all retarded persons are categorized as profoundly retarded, 3.5% as severe, and 6% as moderate. Research has provided us with enough information to be able to *prevent* more than 75 percent of all retardation!

Certainly this is a challenge to which the church must respond.

Many Levels of Retardation

Mentally retarded persons, just as "normal" persons, are individuals with distinct characteristics and abilities. Mentally retarded persons cannot be described in all-inclusive terms. Some are pretty; some are not. Some have astounding memories; others cannot retain the most basic information from day to day. Some communicate extremely well; many cannot speak clearly or at all. Many retarded persons who have not been labeled as such are married, have families, and are gainfully employed.

Five categories or levels have been identified to allow for convenience in describing mentally retarded persons.

Classification and Characteristics

Level	Terms Used	General Level
Borderline	Borderline	Marginally dependent
Mild	Educable Mentally Retarded (EMR) Educable Mentally Handicapped (EMH) Educable	Marginally independent. Lower self-image. More poorly developed motor skills. Shorter attention span. Cannot deal with abstractions. Slower academically. Lower social interests.
Moderate	Trainable Mentally Retarded (TMR) Trainable Mentally Handicapped (TMH) Trainable	Semidependent Require supervision in self-help skills. Often appear "different." One or more physical problems.
Severe	Severely Mentally Retarded (SMR) Severely Mentally Handicapped (SMH) Severely Retarded	Dependent.
Profound	Profoundly Mentally Retarded (PMR) Custodial Mentally Retarded (CMR)	Completely dependent. Unable to care for themselves. Often cannot communicate or walk.

Mental retardation is often confused with mental illness or emotional disturbance. These problems are not the same, although a retarded person can *also* be emotionally disturbed.

17

Differences Between Mental Retardation and Mental Illness

Mental Retardation	Mental Illness
1. Mental retardation refers to limited mental development.	1. Persons at all levels of mental retardation development can experience mental illness. A person who is mentally retarded may also be mentally ill.
2. Mental retardation is a condition that exists from birth or early childhood.	2. Mental illness can occur at any time during a person's life.
3. At present there is no "cure"* for mental retardation, particularly retardation with physical causes. With early intervention about 75 percent of mental retardation can be prevented or improved through medical, educational, or nutritional approaches.	3. Persons with mental illness can often be treated successfully and can recover.

*Until recently the term "cure" was avoided for scientific and emotional reasons. In 1980 an unusual conference was sponsored by the Association for Retarded Citizens—U.S. titled "Mental Retardation: The Search for Cures." During this conference, there was acknowledgement that "cure" was an attainable goal. (See Menolascino in references in Appendix C.)

Mental Retardation Is Not Hopeless

Mentally retarded persons in the United States (prior to the 1960s) were neglected, abused, and treated as subhumans. They were considered deviants; and it was thought, incorrectly, that mental retardation was, to a large extent, hereditary.

Beginning in the 1950s, two major occurrences were responsible for a change in the image of mentally retarded persons.

First was the creation of the National Association for Retarded Children, a private nonprofit, voluntary organization formed and developed by parents of retarded persons and other interested individuals. In the 1970s, the name was changed to the National Association for Retarded Citizens (NARC) to include both children and adults. Now referred to as ARC—US, it has been an advocacy organization, particularly in education, health, prevention, and human rights. It has over 2,000-member units across the country, and anyone can join.

The second reason for change was the work of the late President John F. Kennedy. President Kennedy had a retarded sister. He took steps to help resolve the problem of mental retardation in the United States. His active work was influential in changing mental retardation from a "closet" issue to a matter of public concern.

Over the past twenty years, there has been a steady increase in movies (*Charly*), television productions (*Bill*), books, and other types of media that have mental retardation as their major subject.

Some families are still embarrassed by their retarded members and are reluctant to bring them out in public, but generally there has been a much greater acceptance of mentally retarded persons by the American people.

Now there are many recreational, social, residential, vocational, and educational programs for retarded persons. Most of these programs receive favorable publicity. This may be due to the increasing involvement and activity by laypersons who are beginning to see retarded persons as human beings.

The Sunday School Board
Responds

Beginning in 1962, the Sunday School Board of the Southern Baptist Convention organized to help state conventions and local churches develop Sunday School programs for mentally retarded persons. Doris Monroe pioneered the work while she was an editor of children's materials. Later she became a full-time consultant in the area of mental retardation.

Today, many churches across the country have special programs for children and adults in Sunday School. A special *Special Ministries Resource Kit—Sunday School/Church Training* and other materials are available through The Sunday School Board.

The Church Program Services Special Ministries Unit, Bible Teaching Division, provides workshops and training sessions for those who want to start or develop programs for mentally retarded persons.

Many state conventions conduct conferences for workers with mentally retarded persons, and some have special weekend retreats for mentally retarded persons.

Further, state conventions and local churches are being encouraged to provide a wide range of ministries beyond the Sunday School class (described in more detail in Chapter 6).

Although there are 6½ million mentally retarded persons in the United States, fewer than 1,000 Southern Baptist churches have organized Sunday School special education classes. This estimate is based on the number of *Special Ministries Resources Kits—Sunday School/Church Training* ordered each quarter by Southern Baptist churches and does not include those churches that develop and use other curriculum approaches. More than 36 thousand churches in the Southern Baptist Convention are without a special ministry to mentally retarded persons. What a challenge remains!

---

*Matthew 9:37: "Then saith he unto his disciples,
The harvest truly is plenteous, but the labourers are few."*

Attitudes Are Reflected in Terms

The way we refer to a person often reveals our attitude about that person. Some terms, while not precise, indicate a positive feeling: brilliant, smart, classy. But many terms, even though originally used as medical descriptions, have almost dropped out of professional or lay usage because of the negative connotations they have developed over the years: feebleminded, moron, imbecile, idiot, and defective. Some terms continue to be used even though they are outmoded: mongoloid (Down's Syndrome), retardate (retarded person).

Many families are sensitive about the terms used to refer to their mentally retarded children. An awareness of the least-degrading terms will help in developing an effective ministry. For example, the use of the term "educable mentally retarded" (EMR) is being replaced by the use of "educable mentally handicapped" (EMH) in many public school systems.

Even though the term "exceptional" is technically accurate when referring to mentally retarded persons, it is a term more commonly used when referring to gifted persons.

Terms that emphasize individuality are retarded *person*, retarded *child*, retarded *adult*, retarded *girl*, or retarded *man*—not just *the* retarded. Even more preferred is "person *with* mental retardation," which emphasizes the person, not the problem.

The attitude and language of the Christian ought to be governed by the principle that all persons are human beings and—regardless of physical, mental, or social problems—must be treated as persons who need to be respected and nurtured.

Ethical Issues

Beginning in the late 1960s and increasingly since, a series of ethical problems has gained public attention. First, the dehumanizing conditions of institutions were described in the media. Overcrowding, lack of trained workers, and insufficient funds all brought a public and legal demand for reform.

A concept referred to as "normalization" gained support and helped lead to the decentralizing of institutions.

Normalization is an effort to provide life experiences as closely as possible to those that would be expected if the retarded individual were without a handicap.

About the same time, mandatory public education (often referred to as Public Law 94-142) was implemented across the country. With deinstitutionalization and mandatory public education came some critical ethical issues yet unresolved:

Who can be born?—Abortion is a controversial and emotional issue. Sophisticated tests make it possible to detect chromosomal, physical, biochemical, and mental abnormalities during pregnancy. These tests bring agony to families who are asked to make a decision about continuing or terminating a pregnancy.

Who will be allowed to live?—"Baby Doe" is the term used to refer to mentally retarded and multiple handicapped newborn babies who require surgical corrective measures to make it possible for them to live. Recently, one Baby Doe gained national attention when her parents refused to grant permission for surgery. Consequently, Baby Doe died of starvation. The issue has received much media coverage and debate.

Where will they be allowed to live?—The advent of group homes for mentally retarded persons in community residential settings brought forth a rash of legal suits in an attempt to prevent their establishment. The issue involves nondiscriminating residential rights.

May they marry?—Retarded adults who had lived in institutions much of their lives were suddenly decentralized and placed in various types of community residential settings. Some married and lived in apartment complexes. The issue of marriage between retarded persons has always been controversial, but it clearly is an ethical issue. Do mentally retarded adults have the *right* to marry as other adults?

22

May they have children?—The heart of the issue is this: Should mentally retarded adults have children? Do they have the right to have children?

Of course these ethical issues do not have easy or pat answers. Involved in these five issues are two basic precepts:
• The sanctity of life
• The value of the individual
Stories of success and failure are used to support both sides of each issue. The Christian's response must be based on prayer, serious study, and the question: How would Jesus respond?

Robert Portman

Bills of Rights

"Declaration of General and Special Rights of the Mentally Retarded," originally drafted by the International League of Societies for the Mentally Handicapped in 1968, was adopted by the United Nations General Assembly in 1971. The seven articles of the declaration decreed:

Article I
The mentally retarded person has the same basic rights as other citizens of the same country and same age.

Article II
The mentally retarded person has a right to proper medical care and physical restoration and to such education, training, habilitation, and guidance as will enable him to develop his ability and potential to the fullest possible extent, no matter how severe his degree of disability. No mentally handicapped person should be deprived of such services by reason of the costs involved.

Article III
The mentally retarded person has a right to economic security and to a decent standard of living. He has a right to productive work or to other meaningful occupation.

Article IV
The mentally retarded person has a right to live with his own family or with foster parents, to participate in all aspects of community life, and to be provided with appropriate leisuretime activities. If care in an institution becomes necessary, it should be in surroundings and other circumstances as close to normal living as possible.

Article V
The mentally retarded person has a right to a qualified guardian when this is required to protect his personal well-being and interest. No person rendering direct services to the mentally retarded should also serve as his guardian.

Article VI

The mentally retarded person has a right to protection from exploitation, abuse, and degrading treatment. If accused, he has a right to a fair trial with full recognition being given to his degree of responsibility.

Article VII

Some mentally retarded persons may be unable, due to the severity of their handicap, to exercise for themselves all of their rights in a meaningful way. For others, modification of some or all of these rights is appropriate. The procedure used for modification or denial of rights must contain proper legal safeguards against every form of abuse, must be based on an evaluation of the social capability of the mentally retarded person by qualified experts, and must be subject to periodic reviews and to the right of appeal to higher authorities.[1]

---

[1] R. B. Scheerenberger, A *History of Mental Retardation* (Baltimore: Paul H. Brookes Publishing Co., 1983), pp. 250-251.

Personal Learning Activities

1. What is the estimated number of retarded persons in the United States?
2. Based on a three percent estimate of the population of your city or town, how many retarded persons live in your town?
3. Give a simple general definition of mental retardation.
4. Of the five levels of mental retardation, what is the lowest?
5. "Mongoloid" is an outdated term still in use. What is a more appropriate term?

"And great multitudes came unto him, having
with them those that were lame, blind, dumb,
maimed, and many others, and cast them
down at Jesus' feet; and he healed them"
(Matt. 15:30).

Chapter 2

Why Have a Ministry?

The question, "Why have a ministry?" goes straight to the core of the church's reason for existence. Yet, many people miss the significance of a ministry to mentally retarded persons. They substitute "busy" activities aimed at pleasing the retarded person rather than instilling spiritual truths.

How a teacher, church staff member, or pastor views the retarded person often determines how and to what extent the retarded person develops spiritually.

Jesus Set the Example

Jesus set the model for ministering to the needs of persons with various handicaps. He responded to the needs of lepers; to persons with paralysis; to persons who were lame, blind, deaf, or maimed; and to many other persons with profound problems. Most of these persons were considered hopeless, and their pleas to Jesus were desperate cries for help.

Mental retardation represents a hopeless situation to most people. Many parents are on a quest for the miraculous answer. They seek physical and sensorimotor cures, educational cures, nutritional cures, and behavioral cures.

The church has a spiritual message of hope that must be presented and shared. Jesus set the example.

The Urgent Task

The primary work of the Christian is to nurture persons spiritually—*all* persons. God's message is to be presented to everyone:

- The intellectual "up and outs"
- The poor "down and outs"
- The suffering and dying
- The frustrated and confused
- Persons of all races, nationalities, and colors
- Handicapped and disabled persons

The New Testament message is clear:

> *"Go ye therefore, and teach all nations, baptizing them in the name of the Father, and the Son, and of the Holy Ghost: Teaching them to observe all things whatsoever I have commanded you: and, lo, I am with you alway, even unto the end of the world"* (Matt. 28:19-20).

Yet in some ways the church picks and chooses in its outreach efforts. There is a tendency to reach out to those who will bring quick results, those who can and want to communicate, those who are "normal," those who are not considered absolutely hopeless.

Our task is not to judge and select those whom we believe can benefit from the message of the gospel. It is to present the message to *all* persons.

The church is reluctant to witness and minister to mentally retarded persons because of:

- **Fear**—"Retarded persons can be unpredictable, dangerous."

- **Uneasiness**—"I can't understand what they are trying to say."

- **Pity**—"I feel so sorry for them; I feel like crying."

- **Embarrassment**—"We may offend others or discourage them from coming to our church."

- **Hopelessness**—"Retarded persons do not comprehend spiritual truths."

- **Avoidance**—"They are not accountable and are automatically provided for."

Our Spiritual Weaknesses Mirrored

As our relationships with retarded persons deepen, we begin to recognize human weaknesses that we "normal persons" have.

Retarded Persons	"Normal" Persons
• Express feelings honestly, without embarrassment	• Inhibited, guarded, pretentious
• Openly loving	• Cautious in new friendships
• Trusting	• Pessimistic
• Accept spiritual truths easily and without question	• Prone to question, debate, rationalize

These characteristics of many retarded persons have spiritual counterparts in "normal" persons:

Retarded Persons	"Normal" Persons
• Forgetful	• Forget God's place in their lives
• Poor judgment	• Daily decisions reflect a self-centered, greedy nature
• Hyperactive	• "Busy" lives ignore God
• Self-centered	• Submissive to worldly pleasures

With Ministry Improvement

Often we think that if we ignore a problem, the problem will go away! But with mental retardation, the problem is apt to get worse or certainly more complex.

As parents get older, their concern for continuing care for their retarded son or daughter becomes more pressing. If the church offers no alternative, the parents can only look at secular programs.

If a retarded child is allowed to develop inappropriate behaviors without training for socialization skills, then it becomes so much more difficult to become acceptable to the general public as an adult.

If a retarded person has no dietary restrictions or physical exercise requirements, then obesity will be a problem that affects every other aspect of daily living.

The church's ministry to mentally retarded persons and their families ought to begin as soon as the need is discovered. (See Chapter 6.)

Jesus was always responsive to the immediate need. His church should not do less.

Reminder of Priorities

Just like other special ministries in prisons, hospitals, and nursing homes, the special ministry to mentally retarded persons keeps us aware of the priorities established by Jesus.

Allows Family Ministry

Ministering to a mentally retarded child or adult usually opens a door to opportunities for ministry to other members of the retarded person's family.

Parents who see the enthusiastic, positive, and accepting relationship that is developed between the retarded son or daughter and a teacher, church worker, church staff member, or pastor are more willing to share family needs that are usually kept private and guarded. Some of these needs are as follows:
• Weakened bond in marriage
• Restricted social and friendship opportunities
• Fatigue, both physical and emotional
• Spiritual confusion
• Fear of the future
• Strained relationship of mentally retarded person with other children in the family and community

As one ministers to the retarded person, a closer and trusting relationship develops with the parents and other family members. Such trust is a critical step to an effective witness.

Positive Side Effects

One cannot minister to mentally retarded persons by the example and in the spirit of Jesus without receiving positive side effects:
• Patience
• Empathy
• Sensitivity
• Spiritual self-discipline
• Awareness of needs
• Strong, positive attitudes
• Love for people
• Appreciation for the healing ministry of Jesus
• Strengthened faith

Do Unto Others . . .

"Therefore all things whatsoever ye would that men should do to you, do ye even so to them: for this is the law and the prophets"
(Matt. 7:12).

The Golden Rule sets forth one of the most powerful reasons why we should minister to mentally retarded persons. If I were the mentally retarded person, would I want you to minister to me? Of course!

Yet a ministry to retarded persons is rarely a one-way relationship. Retarded persons can—and do—minister to others in countless ways, especially spiritually.

Consider "The Miracles," a singing group of mildly and moderately mentally retarded persons who are residents at the Baddour Memorial Center in Senatobia, Mississippi. "The Miracles" have performed all over the United States. The singers thrill audiences, not only because they are retarded *and* talented, but also because they have a stirring spiritual message to share.

Consider John Keaton and Jim Sandridge. Both live at home in Virginia. John has Down's Syndrome. His mother encouraged him to learn to read music and play the piano. Every month he goes to a nursing home and plays the piano for the residents. Jim does not have a precise diagnosis. He is a competent piano tuner, plays the organ often for his church's worship service.

There are countless other retarded persons who are purposefully sharing their talents with "normal" groups!

Mentally retarded persons are actually demonstrating the true meaning of the Golden Rule: That love is best expressed *between* persons.

Personal Learning Activities

1. List six reasons for developing a mental retardation ministry.

2. Give six reasons why churches are reluctant to develop a mental retardation ministry.

3. Choose one of these reasons, and describe your feelings about it.

4. What is a critical step in developing an effective ministry to parents and other family members?

The Face Beyond

Olson Huff, MD
Asheville, NC

I don't recall his name. He always sat rigidly in his wheelchair, backed up against the wall, white enameled steel beds surrounding him like the bars of a prison. He cared little for the movies I brought from the university film library and held back from the banter and rowdy play of the other children, even those in wheelchairs like his own. His dark eyes burned when I dared look at him, and I knew that he needed more from me than movies. I pretended not to notice, finding the other side of the room more comfortable. . . . That was years ago and I don't recall his name. But like a flicker of blue sky pushing through gray clouds, my mind is occasionally stimulated by the memory of his searching eyes, and I am challenged anew. Challenged to be the man whose presence can release some of the fear and hurt in the young who see me daily, and challenged to reassure them that they no longer need to search beyond my face to find one who is a friend.

From the Journal of the American Medical Association, March 16, 1984, Volume 251, p. 1423. © 1984, American Medical Association.

Chapter 3

Starting a Ministry for Mentally Retarded Persons

Starting a ministry for mentally retarded persons requires the same preparation as it does for any other ministry:

- Make a commitment
- Pray for direction
- Seek biblical insight
- Educate yourself
- Educate the pastor
- Educate the congregation
- Recruit and train teachers
- Develop an outreach program
- Prepare curriculum
- Prepare the room
- Set a date and start!

Make a Commitment

A commitment to a task or ministry precedes its becoming a reality. The Bible has countless examples of commitments made by outstanding men and women of God.

Without a commitment, a ministry is like any other well-intentioned secular service that has no spiritual base.

Pray for Direction

A Christian committed to the ministry of mental retardation enters into a regular time for prayer, giving praise, and seeking direction. True prayer—that which bears fruit—is a spiritual skill requiring discipline, a receptive spirit, and a willingness to follow the leading of God's Spirit. Discipline means practice; a receptive spirit is one that listens to God; and a willingness to follow God's leading calls for an adventurous faith.

- Is there a specific time of each day set aside for prayer?
- Is prayer time hurried?
- Is prayer specific? Does it include names and situations?
- Is there praise in prayer?

Nancy Robinson

Seek Biblical Insight

We speak to God through prayer. Often God speaks to us through His Word. Seeking God's leading through regular individualized Bible study can be an adventure for Christians. Many good Bible study plans are appropriate for individual study, depending on spiritual maturity and personal spiritual needs.

Educate Yourself

God expects us to be competent and knowledgeable in our commitment. A ministry to mentally retarded persons and their families demands that a person be informed about mental retardation.

> *"Study to shew thyself approved unto God, a workman that needeth not to be ashamed, rightly dividing the word of truth"* (2 Tim. 2:15).

Just as doctors, lawyers, business persons, and teachers work hard to become and stay informed, so workers with mentally retarded persons should be knowledgeable about the conditions and the persons with whom they work.

How does one become informed? There are numerous ways.

Read about mental retardation.—Although it was once difficult to find up-to-date information about mental retardation, many publications now include practical information about the problems and its many related facets.
- Women's magazines
- Books (both lay and professional)
- Government publications
- Specialized publications
- Brochures and reports from voluntary organizations

Watch documentary films and other audiovisual presentations.—Television programming now includes informative documentaries about mental retardation and other related handicapping conditions. Universities and other educational and voluntary organizations offer a wide range of films, filmstrips, and cassette titles that are free or inexpensive.

Talk to parents of mentally retarded persons.—It has been suggested that parents of retarded children deserve an honorary doctoral degree! Certainly 24-hour care of a retarded child helps a parent develop an impressive reservoir of knowledge and experience about the problem of mental retardation. Arrange to talk to parents of retarded persons. Ask them what methods they use to educate and train their children. Parents are eager to share this knowledge.

Training Conferences.—State convention offices and the Sunday School Board conduct training conferences that include workshops for those who work with mentally retarded persons.

Public Libraries.—Public libraries carry many of the most recent titles of publications about mental retardation. If they do not, request that they do so.

Governmental Publications.—The United States Department of Education, Washington, DC, carries many titles of publications about mental retardation and other handicapping conditions. Many are free.

University Courses.—Your state universities or private colleges may have a special education curriculum. Contact the special education department, and ask for the list of media used in various courses. Some of these may be appropriate for purchase by the local church's media library.

Private Voluntary Organizations.—Reading material and audiovisual items are available through various voluntary organizations. (See Appendix A.)

Meetings.—Local or county chapters of private voluntary organizations hold regular meetings at which there are special speakers and topics that will be of interest and value to you. Contact them and ask for information about their meetings and membership costs.

Discussion with Authorities.—Experts in the field of mental retardation are excellent resources about the latest information. Make an appointment and go prepared to ask specific, relevant questions of the following persons:

• **Governmental representative.**—Local, state, and federal levels. Departments of Mental Retardation, Education, Public Health and Human Services are examples.

• **Colleges and universities.**—Instructors in special education.

• **Voluntary organizations.**—The executive director or his representative.

• **Churches with established and successful programs.**—The pastor, minister of education, or special education department teacher.

• **Newspapers and magazines.**—Many current articles and human interest stories are published in a wide variety of newspapers and magazines. Write or contact the writers.

• **Talk with Professional Workers.**—Public and private school teachers of special education classes are good resources of information. (If you live near a university or college that has a special education department, make an appointment to speak to one or more of the instructors. Ask for recommended reading.)

• **Finally, Seek Information from Retarded Persons.**—Those who can communicate can help you decide about the appropriateness of material. "Which do you like better, John? This . . . or this? Which would you rather do? Do you want to keep doing this, or do you want to do something else?"

Educate the Pastor

The most important person in the development of a mental retardation ministry within a church is the pastor. Many pastors do not know much about mental retardation. Introduce him to a retarded person. Seek to educate the pastor and other church staff members.

1. Make an Appointment with the Pastor.—Let him know of your interest in developing a ministry to mentally retarded persons. Do not carry on a lengthy discussion. Do not press for a commitment. Do not ask him to do anything except listen to you. Tell him why you want to do something about the problem. Tell him why something needs to be done. Tell him what spiritual and outreach results can take place with an ongoing, caring ministry.

2. Leave a few selected items.—Encourage a pastor to read and share these with his staff or other interested key church workers. Recommended are the following:
- *Your Church and the Mentally Retarded* (available through the state Sunday School office)
- *The Problem of Mental Retardation* (Department of Health, Education, and Welfare, Washington, DC 20201)

- *Ministering to Persons with Mental Retardation and Their Families* by Gene Nabi (available through your Baptist Book Store)

3. Offer Your Help.—Ask the pastor what he would like for you to do. Be prepared to tell him what needs to be done and how, if he asks.

4. Recommend or Leave a Publication.—This will allow him to study the problem at his convenience. Six titles are suggested:
- *Ethical Issues in Mental Retardation—Tragic Choices/Living Hope* by David F. and Victoria S. Allen. Nashville: Abingdon Press, 1979
- *We Have Been There* compiled by Terrell Dougan, Lyn Isbell, and Patricia Vyas. Nashville: Abingdon Press, 1983
- *Hope for the Families* by Robert Perske. Nashville: Abingdon Press, 1981
- *New Life in the Neighborhood* by Robert Perske. Nashville: Abingdon Press, 1981
- *Come Care with Me* by Lottie R. Crim. Nashville: Broadman Press, 1983
- *No Pat Answers* by Eugenia Price. Grand Rapids: Zondervan Books, 1972
- *Mental Retardation Past and Present.* President's Committee on Mental Retardation. (To secure this free report, write: President's Committee on Mental Retardation, Washington, DC 20201)

5. What Next?—Before you conclude the discussion, know what the next step is. Another meeting with the pastor? When? Discussion with other church staff members or church leadership (Sunday School department director, a deacon or chairman of the deacons, WMU president, Church Training director)?

6. Prayer.—Conclude your discussion with a prayer. You may wish to ask the pastor to lead.

It is best to approach the pastor on a one-to-one basis or with no more than one other person. Keep this from seeming to be a committee meeting. (The pastor has more than his share!) Keep it personal.

Educate the Congregation

If a congregation is aware of the need for a ministry to mentally retarded persons and their families and has been educated about mental retardation, the outreach results will be significant.

Congregations need to be taught how to relate to families with mentally retarded members. Too often a fear of saying the wrong words keeps committed Christians from ministering effectively to these families.

Several simple steps will help educate a congregation:

1. Ask the pastor to announce and indicate his support for the special education ministry. He may even wish to preach a sermon on the subject!

2. March is Mental Retardation Month and is a good time to include a special insert in the weekly bulletin. The Sunday School Board can furnish samples.

3. A ten-minute 75-frame, color filmstrip *Guiding the Retarded in Chrisitan Living and Learning* with accompanying cassette could be shown to the congregation during Mental Retardation Month. This filmstrip (4435-71) may be secured from your nearest Baptist Book Store. State conventions may also have helpful resources.

4. Prepare and offer to present a brief program on mental retardation to any church group (Sunday School, Church Training, WMU, Deacons).

5. Submit regular (monthly or quarterly) news for the church paper or bulletin, telling of progress and needs.

6. Especially effective is a brief testimonial from a parent about the special education program.

7. If possible, have the special education department present a program to demonstrate some of the results of the church's ministry.

8. Denominational resources may be secured from the associational or state Sunday School offices. At the Convention level, the Special Ministries Unit, Bible Teaching Division of The Sunday School Board, is available for help in developing training programs and for consultation in specialized problems.

Be prepared to respond to members of the congregation who ask what they can do to help. Examples include the following: (1) transportation needs; (2) help with special annual events (such as Christmas, Thanksgiving, special education banquet, Easter); (3) special entertainment by persons who can sing, play musical instruments, put on puppet shows; and (4) contributions of special items needed by the Special Education Department (furniture, art and crafts supplies, records, books, and other teaching items).

Think of ways in which there can be a two-way ministry between the congregation and the retarded persons!

• Higher functioning adult retarded persons can assist in ushering and collecting the offering.

• Many retarded persons are talented musically and can

present special music in solos, groups, and instruments.
- Those who can read well can read the Scripture passage during the worship service on special occasions.

The Miracles,
Baddour Memorial Center

- Many retarded persons are capable of vocal prayers that are honest, to the point, and poignant.
- There are many church functions that can be carried out effectively by retarded persons: Greeting, ushering, distributing material, food preparation, and maintenance.
- Retarded persons can visit nursing homes and retirement centers with another experienced visitation team member.
- Some retarded persons can work as helpers.
- Some persons, carefully selected and trained, can function as workers in Preschool and Children's departments.

Recruit and Train Teachers

A common concern in starting and developing a ministry to mentally retarded persons and their families is the availability of competent and qualified teachers.

There is a mistaken notion that those who teach retarded persons must have some mysterious or rare qualities. Characteristics of a good teacher of mentally retarded persons are the same as those of *any* good teacher:
- Be a committed and mature Christian.
- Have a calling to teach.
- Be willing to study and learn. (See Chapter 3, "Educate Yourself.")
- Be dependable.
- Be willing to plan and prepare.
- Be committed to ministry to the whole family.

Many people believe that the basic requirements to teach retarded persons are love and patience. These are important qualities, but far more is involved in becoming a competent teacher.

A good teacher or a potential teacher:
- Feels a calling or a strong desire to teach.
- Is willing to prepare.
- Completes *Reaching and Teaching Mentally Retarded Persons* by Doris Monroe (now out of print) or *Ministering to Persons with Mental Retardation and Their Families* by Gene Nabi.

Develop an Outreach Program

Without members in the special education program, there can be no ministry. An organized outreach program is vital to a growing, effective ministry.
(See Chapter 4 for additional information.)

Prepare Curriculum

Getting the names of prospects to visit and enroll is only part of the ministry. The curriculum should create a continuing desire to come. Because each department is likely to have persons at different ages and ability, no one approach can be used for everyone. Some retarded persons can read, communicate clearly, and socialize with little difficulty. Others cannot. These differences require creative ways to teach the same spiritual truths.
(Chapter 7 tells how to develop and use curriculum. Remember, curriculum refers to any teaching or learning aid, not just printed material.)

Prepare the Room

The type and location of the classroom is important.
Is the classroom located on a ground-level floor?
Is the classroom easily accessible to wheelchairs?
Is there a bathroom in the classroom or nearby?
Are there windows?
The classroom should be bright and cheerful. The walls should not be too "busy," and the room should be arranged to accommodate the lesson and its goals.
Furniture should be selected according to the ages and sizes of the members. The room helps set the mood and atmosphere and prepares the class members for learning experiences. In addition, it helps the teacher feel prepared and ready to teach.

47

Set a Date and Start!

All the preceding preparation activities are of no value if the program does not get started! Rarely will there be a feeling that "everything has been done, and we are ready to begin." It is necessary to set a date and start on that date. How many retarded persons should be enrolled before a program can start? One! Simply activating the program will attract enrollments, but seeking other enrollees should be a continuing part of the process. (See Chapter 4, "Outreach.")

Personal Learning Activities

1. What do you consider the most important step in starting a mental retardation ministry? Why?
2. How and where can a person become informed about mental retardation?
3. Why do you think the pastor of a church needs to be knowledgeable about mental retardation?
4. What qualities should a teacher of retarded persons have?
5. In your own words, describe an "ideal" classroom.

HEROISM

Parents of persons with mental retardation are unsung heroes in the finest sense. Theirs is a commitment and dedication of the highest order: caring and unselfishly serving the critical needs of a human being.

The finest hour for traditional heroes is brief and momentary:

- The astronaut who walks on the moon.
- The fire fighter who saves a child from a burning building.
- The young person who rescues his drowning sister.
- The person who prevents the death of a person through immediate first aid.

But the "finest hour" for the parent of a child or adult with mental retardation is twenty-four hours a day for a lifetime.

THAT'S HEROISM!

Chapter 4

Outreach

The key to a growing church ministry to retarded persons and their families is an active outreach program.

Most families with mentally retarded members will not make the effort to seek out a church with a mental retardation ministry for three main reasons:

1. Not going to church is easier for them.
2. They do not want to burden the church with the retarded person.
3. They feel guilty or embarrassed.

For these reasons, the church should develop an aggressive outreach program. Families should be convinced that their handicapped children are wanted.

Because of the overprotective nature of many families with retarded members, it may seem that few retarded persons are in the community. Don't forget the statistics presented in Chapter 1. Retarded persons are out there!

Reasons for Not Developing an Outreach Ministry

Consider these reasons often given for *not* developing a ministry to mentally retarded persons and their families:

- "We do not have any mentally retarded persons in our church community."
- "Another local church already offers a program."
- "We have asked some parents, and they do not seem to be interested."
- "We made an announcement about starting a class, but no one responded."

An active outreach program can overcome all these reasons

for not developing a program for mentally retarded persons and their families.

Mentally retarded persons may not be visible in a community for various reasons, *but they are there!*

Just to tell parents about the class is not enough. Parents must be *encouraged and urged* to enroll their son or daughter because of their reluctance to be a burden to anyone. Several telephone calls and personal visits may be required before parents are convinced that you are serious.

Even if a program is offered in another church, other churches may also need a program.

Announcements are not the most effective method of enrolling mentally retarded persons. Announcements are tools in making it known that a program is available.

Seven Outreach Methods

Personal visitation is the most effective means of outreach. Seven possible outreach methods are listed here:

1. *Ask known parents of retarded persons.*—Each parent knows other parents, and those parents know others. Taking advantage of the "domino effect" will provide a large prospect list.

2. *A good outreach source can be found in public special education schools and classes.*—Retarded persons may attend public schools until twenty-two years of age. Ask that your notice be sent to each family. Attend PTA meetings and announce your church's program. Interested parents will want to take advantage. Secure names, phone numbers, and addresses so a follow-up can be made.

3. *News releases and radio public service announcements.*—These releases are excellent methods of reaching a large population.

The following is a sample news release that can be used as an outreach instrument. It can be changed to fit special situations.

First Baptist Church

Seventh and Broadway
Nashville Tennessee 37203
(615) 256-5168

DATE:_____   CONTACT PERSON:_____

FOR IMMEDIATE RELEASE

NEW PROGRAM FOR MENTALLY HANDICAPPED PERSONS

First Baptist Church, Nashville, has announced that a new
program for mentally handicapped persons will be started on
_____(date)_____ and will be held each Sunday from ___(time)___
to ___(time)___.

A wide variety of activities will be provided, including art,
music, crafts, Bible stories, games and other socialization
activities.

There is no charge for this program. For more details,
contact __(name of special education leader)__ at _(church phone)_.

"The church with a heart in the heart of Nashville"

Type the release on church letterhead. Weekly and
community newspapers are usually more receptive to these
releases than the metropolitan papers. If possible, submit a
sharp black and white glossy photo that can be used as a
captioned photo.

Be alert to the many stories that can be submitted throughout the year, but don't wear out your welcome! Some topic examples:

1. New Program for Mentally Handicapped Persons
2. Program for Mentally Handicapped Persons to Expand
3. Local Persons Participate in Special Olympics
4. First Baptist Church Recognizes Special Olympics Winners
5. Special Education Department Celebrates Christmas (or other special days)

Other human interest stories based on personalities—such as teachers, members, families—can be appropriate for the local newspaper. Ask for guidelines from the publication's editor.

4. Local association for retarded citizens.—The ARC is always cooperative in distributing information about church programs. Some ARC's have religious nurture committees that make available a listing of churches with programs. Your church should be added to the list. In addition, join the ARC and attend membership meetings where you can announce your church's program and talk individually to interested parents. Emphasize that the program is open to all persons.

5. Prepare and distribute a brochure about your church's program.—The brochure need not be expensive, but it should be informative and attractive. Seek cooperation from high-density traffic places—such as grocery stores, beauty and barber shops, small businesses, and banks—to display the brochure.

6. Television and radio interviews.—These interviews will bring responses to your invitation to visit your program. The person who is interviewed should be knowledgeable and articulate.

7. Ask the congregation.—Members will give names, phone numbers, and addresses of handicapped persons that they know. Follow up with a telephone call and a personal visit. Use the Individual Information Sheet as a guide:

Date _____

INDIVIDUAL INFORMATION SHEET

Name _____Date enrolled _____
Address _____
Phone _____Age _____ Date of birth _____
Parents' names _____
Parents' address (if different from above):
_____

Father a Christian? _____ If yes, what church? _____
Mother a Christian? _____ If yes, what church? _____
Father's occupation _____Where? _____
Mother's occupation _____Where? _____
Where to contact parents during Sunday session:
_____

Brothers? _____ Names and ages _____
Sisters? _____ Names and ages _____
House parent or guardian's name _____
Does member attend: Public school _____Private school _____
Adult activity center _____Sheltered workshop _____Others

Name of above _____
Physical disability? _____ Describe _____
Medical problems? _____ Describe _____
Seizures? _____Diabetic? _____Allergies? _____
Medication? _____ Describe _____
Food restrictions? _____

Special interests
   Pets (names) _____
   Leisuretime activities: _____
   Likes music? _____ Can sing? _____

Special dislikes: _____
_____

Abilities: Can communicate clearly? _____Can read? _____
             Level? _____Can write? _____Level?_____
             Can count? _____ Can tell colors? _____

55

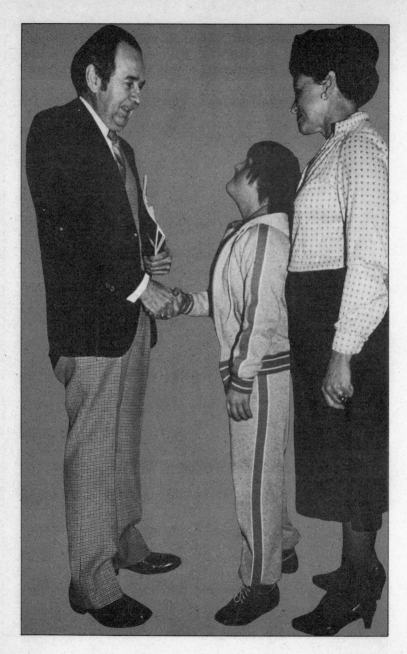

Visitation Is Personal, Powerful

The act of visiting is in itself a personal and powerful demonstration of care.

Visitation is an opportunity to:
- Express interest in the retarded person and his/her family.
- Demonstrate God's love in tangible ways.
- Learn more about the various needs of the family.
- Respond to questions about the church and its ministries.
- Promote the church's ministry to retarded persons in an enthusiastic way.

Some guidelines regarding visitation include:

- Prayer in advance of the visit. Prayer should be specific.
- An appointment made to visit. It should be convenient to the family.
- Conversation should be relaxed and guided.
- Positive statements should be made about the retarded person.
- Personal invitations to all members of the family.

Personal Learning Activities

1. Why do some families with retarded members not attend church?
2. What can be done to convince parents that their retarded son or daughter is welcome at your church?
3. What is the most effective means of outreach?
4. List four outreach methods for locating and attracting families with retarded members to your church.
5. What do you think is the greatest problem in locating retarded persons in your community or town?
6. If your church does not have an organized mental retardation ministry, name two prospects for starting a ministry. If there is a ministry, what can be done to increase its outreach program?

Learning requires good questions. Teaching requires good answers.[1]

---

[1]William L. Hendricks, A *Theology for Children* (Nashville: Broadman Press, 1980), p. 21.

Chapter 5

Recruiting and Training Teachers

Who Makes a Good Teacher?

Some people think that the primary requirements for a teacher of mentally retarded persons are patience and love. While these characteristics are essential for any good teacher, much more is required to teach retarded persons effectively.

A Mature Christian.—Only a mature Christian can minister spiritually to retarded persons. Seeking any other person, even though that person is qualified as a teacher or professional worker, would defeat the purpose of a mental retardation ministry within the church.

A Competent Person.—Information about mental retardation is increasing rapidly because of research and more sophisticated approaches in the field of education. The leader of mentally retarded persons must be informed about the changes. For the new or inexperienced teacher, these books are recommended for a basic understanding of teaching techniques. Although these titles emphasize age groups, the teaching principles can be applied to mentally retarded persons of differing ages.
- *Reaching and Teaching Mentally Retarded Persons* by Doris Monroe (now out of print, but may still be available)
- *Understanding Today's Preschoolers* by Sybil Waldrop
- *Understanding Today's Children* by Max Price
- *Guiding Children* by Elsie Rives and Margaret Sharp

For the experienced teacher and those who have worked with retarded persons, these additional titles are recommended:
• *When Can a Child Believe?* by Eugene Chamberlain
• A *Theology for Children* by William Hendricks
• *Leading the Mentally Retarded in Worship* by Terry Welborn and Gene Williams
(See Appendix C for a recommended reading list.)

A *Comfortable Person*.—Some persons, for various reasons, do not feel at ease around handicapped persons, even after adequate time for adjustment. Persons who work with retarded persons should feel comfortable in this ministry. As one becomes familiar with each retarded person, individual strengths and weaknesses are learned. What at first was unintelligible speech becomes understandable. Likes and dislikes become known. Gradually a warm and sharing friendship develops.

A *Disciplined* Person.—Self-discipline is of great importance to the teacher who is continually developing skills. The teacher of retarded persons must set goals; develop schedules; coordinate activities; and prepare for future programs, events, and activities. All this requires regular self-discipline.

Preparation for the next Sunday's lesson (*Special Ministries Resource Kit—Sunday School/Church Training*) should start on the preceding Sunday. The weekly preparation schedule should include lesson study, Bible study, prayer, and outreach activities.
• *Lesson study*—Read the leadership guide at least three times during the week. What specific message does it contain for your individual members?
• *Bible Study*—Read the Bible story in your Bible; and, if appropriate, read the chapter that comes before and after it.
• *Prayer*—Pray for each class member and his specific needs.
• *Outreach activities*—Plan telephone calls and visits to members and their families.

This outreach schedule may be set up to fit various situations, but it is important to *have* a schedule.

Discipline also includes personal spiritual development—including Bible study, prayer, meditation, and purposeful witnessing. **The Bible contains the same truths for retarded persons as it does for other persons.** A deepening familiarity with the Bible is essential to teachers of retarded persons. There are numerous Bible study plans. Select the one that meets your needs.

As the teacher studies the Bible—whatever the method—there should always be an anticipation of the specific truths that the Scripture holds for retarded persons and their families.

Also there should be the question, "How would I tell or translate this passage or story to my class?"

Some retarded persons can grasp abstract words and symbolic messages. They need the message clear and relevant, just as all persons do! (See "Mental Retardation and Conversion," Chapter 8, "Crystal Clear Clarification.")

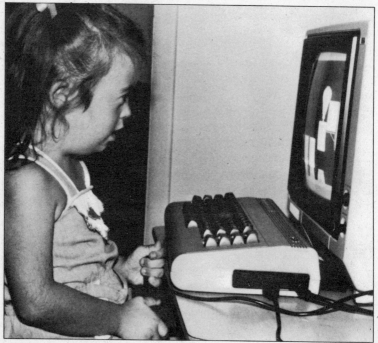

Sister Patricia Connolly

Where Can Good Teachers Be Found?

Everywhere! Consider:
- Former teachers.
- Active teachers in all departments. Some may want a new challenge.
- Mature Christian adults without teaching experience.
- College students.
- Senior adults.
- VBS teachers.
- Church Training leaders.

Should Parents Teach?

Should parents of retarded persons be recruited as teachers?

No—if the parent needs the social and spiritual nurture of his or her peer group.

No—if the parent would be the teacher of his or her child.

Yes—if the parent is a mature Christian who has an active circle of Christian friends.

Yes—if the parent's son or daughter lives away from home and the parent feels a commitment to minister in the area of mental retardation.

Yes—if the parent's son or daughter is deceased and the parent feels a commitment to minister in the area of mental retardation.

Yes—if the parent would not be involved in a direct relationship with his or her son or daughter.

Other teachers in the department may feel inhibited in their relationship with a fellow teacher's son or daughter and may be reluctant to manage behavior in the most appropriate manner.

Who Does Not Make a Good Teacher?

Persons with certain types of personality traits do not make good teachers.

- Those who are emotionally unstable.
- Those who are just "shopping" for somewhere to serve.
- Those who agree to teach but do not have a sense of enthusiasm or commitment.

Prepare the Prospective Teacher

Require the prospective teacher to visit in the department for several Sundays so he will get a good understanding of what is required and can be evaluated in the special education atmosphere.

Have several conferences with the prospective teacher to make certain that the responsibilities are fully understood.

Follow the leading of God in seeking and recruiting teachers.
- Let people know of the need.
- Always be alert to recognizing a prospect.
- Pray before you approach a prospect.
- Don't pressure a prospect into accepting.

After Enlistment, Train

Once a teacher has been enlisted, arrange for training opportunities.

Contact your associational and state convention offices about upcoming training programs and conferences for special education teachers.

Especially helpful are the conferences conducted during the summer Sunday School Leadership Weeks at Glorieta and Ridgecrest. Contact your local church office for the schedule. Make reservations at the earliest possible time!

Other special conferences are held at state-sponsored retreats and are extremely helpful in gaining new perspective and learning new methods in working with mentally retarded persons.

Encourage all teachers to participate regularly in training conferences.

Resources and References

Information abounds about mental retardation and how to work with mentally retarded persons.

Because there are many levels of retarded persons, many resources must be *adapted* to the needs of individuals.

A good basic reference is *Reaching and Teaching Mentally Retarded Persons* by Doris Monroe. It is out of print now, but copies may still be available through local Baptist Book Stores or in your church media library.

The *Special Ministries Resource Kit—Sunday School/Church Training* is a quarterly kit used with retarded persons at all functioning levels. With adaptations, the kit can meet the needs of those who have special or unusual problems. Chapter 9, "Curriculum," offers more information on this kit.

See Appendix C for other resources and references.

Personal Learning Activity

1. Name three characteristics of a good special education Sunday School teacher.

2. Name two types of personality traits not found in good teachers.

3. Give three reasons that the parent of a retarded person should be recruited to teach in a special education department.

It is not like having a death in the family, when people come together to grieve and draw comfort from the presence of friends and family. Learning that one's child is "not normal" is a lonely experience; having such a child tends to thrust the parents outside the mainstream of help, comfort, and advice. Uncommon problems cannot be shared with next-door neighbors. Friends and relatives feel, and often are, ill qualified to advise or assist. The usual sources of professional help, like one's physician, may seem inappropriate. The parent himself may feel some alienation from the "normal" world around him.[1]

[1]Kathryn A. Gorham, Charlotte Desjardins, Ruth Page, Eugene Pettes and Barbara Scheiber, "Effect on Parents" in *Issues in the Classification of Children*, © 1974. Volume 2, Chapter 20, page 156, edited by Nicholas Hobbs.

Chapter 6

Ministering to the Family

Mental Retardation Has a Powerful Influence

The presence of a mentally retarded person in a family affects every aspect of every other member's life. Immediate family members—parents, siblings, grandparents—are affected and influenced by the retarded person. Depending on the severity:
- Parents are limited in their social activities.
- Siblings are embarrassed to bring friends home.
- Weaknesses in a marriage may be aggravated.
- Medical and educational costs may place a strain on the family budget.

Those who work with and teach mentally retarded persons can significantly increase the scope of their ministry by including the families of retarded persons.

Families move, mothers seek employment, fathers seek a second job, brothers and sisters train for a special education career—because of their relationship to a retarded person.

Sometimes there are good results: Marriages may be strengthened; family members may become more sensitive and loving; friends may increase the depth of their relationships to the family; churches may respond to the spiritual, social, and emotional needs of the family members.

There can also be bad results: Marriage bonds may be weakened, sometimes leading to separation and divorce; family members may refuse to accept the fact that there is a handicap; brothers and sisters may leave the family as soon as possible; and churches may neglect the family and its critical needs.

Wide Range of Family Attitudes

Attitudes of families have a wide range. Some of these are listed here:
- Extremely proud and "show off" the retarded member.
- Angry and embarrassed.
- Hesitate to talk or refer to the retarded members for fear of burdening friends.
- Embarrassed to the extent that they refuse to develop normal and healthy social relationships.
- Hurt, discouraged, confused, unable to function in daily activities.

Concerns of the family include the following:
- How can we train the child to learn as much as possible?

- Where should he go to school?
- Should we move to another city for his benefit?
- What will happen if he wanders away and gets lost?
- As the child becomes an adult, will there be understanding by those who meet him?
- What will he do during the summer while school is out?

By far, the most urgent concern is this: "What will happen to our retarded child if we die or if we are permanently disabled?"

In all of these concerns, the church should be involved and supportive. It should become familiar with the family and its status.

First, before a ministry can be developed, there needs to be a special familiarity with the members of the family.

Classical Reactions of the Family

There is a process through which families go in their responses to the retarded member:

- **Shock**—Whether the diagnosis is sudden (at birth) or gradual (upon evaluation in the first grade), having a family member labeled "mentally retarded" is a shocking experience for the members of the family. Classical questions are asked:
  Why me?
  Why does this happen?
  What can be done?
  Can I pray for a miracle?
  What will happen after death?

- **Priorities Change**—What once was considered important may not be so now. Often there is a lack of feeling about many former priorities. The only urgency is that of caring for the retarded child. The family's relationships to the church may change during this period. A loss of interest in active church participation may be rationalized, using the retarded person as the excuse. "It is too much of a problem to get Johnny ready to come to Sunday School and church. Maybe next Sunday."

- **Denial and Anger**—"My child is *not* retarded, just slow. What does the doctor really know about my child? Doctors have made many mistakes. This would not have happened if the doctor had . . . ."

- **Conflict Between Reality and Hopes**—Maybe there is a way to correct this problem, think the parents as they become extremely sensitive and receptive to "miracle treatments." This is a time when parents search for cures and treatments. Money is no factor; nor is family or other relationships. There is a race with time. "We must find the answer soon. The older our child gets, the less the chance for a cure."

- **Guilt Sets In**—Whose fault is this? Whose side of the family has similar or other birth problems? Did the mother not care for herself during pregnancy? Did the father not help enough with household chores? Were there family problems that caused undue worry by the mother? During this period, existing weaknesses in the family are magnified and distorted. Lack of trust between the mother and the father may erupt into open hostility.

- **Depression, Grief Take Over**—The feelings of depression over the retarded child resemble or are the same as grief experienced over the actual loss of a loved one. Because friends—and Christian friends—do not know what to say or how to relate to this "living grief," there is a separation or avoidance. The parents interpret this as lack of care or interest, and the possibility for developing a healing ministry is reduced.

- **Acceptance**—The cures and miracles have been sought. There may have been some improvement but no cure. The family begins to realize and accept the problem as a permanent one. Acceptance can be positive or negative. If positive, the family is receptive to the ministry of the church. If negative, the family may be hostile to all the "do-gooders."

- **Coming to Terms**—Acceptance of the reality of a retarded child is not enough. It may take years and years for families to "come to terms" with their child's retardation, to learn to cope with the daily chores of caring for a retarded person, and to put that reality in proper perspective among all the other family realities.
  If spouses or other children are neglected because of the retarded family member or if the family's spiritual growth is ignored, then it is likely that the process of "coming to terms" is not taking place. If the parents or family take a vacation away from the retarded member, there should not be a guilt feeling. Regular times of renewal should be routine. The church can provide respite ("relief") care during these critical times.

How Can the Church Minister?

Church members can minister to families with a retarded member in simple yet effective ways.

- **Listen**—At times a hurt and confused parent needs to verbalize his or her thoughts and feelings. A Christian friend can minister often just by listening.

- **Speak**—A few words of truth offered in a loving manner may correct wrong beliefs or negative attitudes. For example, if the parent says, "Why has God done this to me?" an adequate response is this: "God did not do this to you. He is a loving God." It is of little value to debate issues that are on an emotional plane.

- **Visit**—A visit demonstrates your interest and concern and should be preceded with prayer. Call in advance to arrange for the visit. Be natural in conversation; and, if there is a desire to discuss a problem, be receptive and listen. Do not be afraid to say "I do not know" if you cannot answer a question.

- **Continue**—If one visit demonstrates your interest and concern, subsequent visits seal it with Christian love. Fellowship develops with time and makes it possible to share feelings of pain.

- **Make Up**—A sincere Christian apology will strengthen the weakened ministry: "I am so sorry I have neglected our friendship lately. I just did not know what to say. Tell me how you are feeling."

- **Loosen Up**—A relaxed, informal ministry is best. Natural humor, honest sharing, and a warm and receptive relationship will help find the source and level of pain.

- **Become Informed**—Become knowledgeable about the problem of mental retardation so your ministry can be more effective. Talk to teachers, other parents, and professional workers. Find out what help is available and where. Is there a local association for retarded citizens? Are there churches with an active special education ministry? Is there an outstanding Christian parent of a retarded child who could provide counsel?

The High Cost of a Personal Ministry

Active, effective ministers should be empathetic. They share the feelings of frustration and pain. But, if they wish to remain effective, care must be taken not to become overly involved. The goal of ministering is to help a person in grief to help himself and to develop a strong deepening relationship with God.

Some Personal Ways to Minister

These ways to minister are suggested:
- Visit.
- Call on the phone for a brief chat.
- Offer to babysit or stay with the retarded person to allow the parents a night out.
- If appropriate, take the retarded person out for a meal, a movie, or some other special occasion.
- Encourage the mother to do constructive activities while the retarded child is at school. For example, encourage her to enroll in a crafts course, attend a Bible study group, enroll in an exercise group, or develop personal talents or artistic skills.
- Encourage the father to socialize with other men and participate in his favorite sport, such as bowling, golfing, or fishing. Invite him to church functions for men.
- Offer to provide respite care for the child; that is, a weekend, a week, or longer to give the family relief.

Theological Questions of Mental Retardation

For the most part, dealing with mental retardation is a grief process and requires a grief ministry. Most parents and family members come into direct confrontation with four basic theological questions:
- Why me?
- Who made it this way?
- What now?
- Where after death?

Without dealing with these questions, families will be unable to develop a growing and deepening relationship with God.

One person received these answers in his spiritual quest:

- **Why Me?**—It isn't just me. There are 6½ million others who are mentally retarded. I wasn't singled out. There are many causes of mental retardation. God is not one of the causes.

- **Who Made It This Way?**—God did not. He intended for man to live in a close, loving relationship with his Creator. There are 250-350 causes of mental retardation. Some are results of a sinful world; some are not.

- **What Now?**—It depends on a close relationship to God, who can make all things work for good. I must work actively to make the best possible life for my retarded child and for other children and their families.

- **What After Death?**—God is big enough to handle the eternal welfare of a retarded person. My task is to provide continuing spiritual nurture to my child through my own ministry and the ministry of my church. (See Chapter 8, "Safe, Saved, Lost.")

Problems of Parents

Depending on the severity of retardation, parents have a varied range of problems. The more severe the mental retardation, the more critical and urgent the problems.

Physical Problems.—Parents who have severely or profoundly retarded children are more prone to be tired physically. Their lives revolve around the welfare of their children.

How the Church Can Help. The church can:
- Provide a sitter service to allow the parent or parents time away to shop or visit.
- Provide a respite (relief) service for twenty-four hours, for a weekend, or for a week or longer to allow the parents to take a vacation.
- Provide help to do household chores.
- Take over a cooked meal.
- Provide a Christian support group at church for persons with mentally retarded members.
- Encourage the parents to get enjoyable physical exercise—jogging, walking, bicycling, bowling, tennis—while a sitter

service is provided.
- Perhaps a full day of rest and lazy relaxation would be a remedy in itself.

Emotional Problems.—Emotional energy is often drained in parents who have more severe problems to contend with in their retarded children. If the prognosis for the retarded person is poor or fatal, parents live from day to day in a sort of modified crisis, expecting the worst—but hoping for a miracle!

↓

How the Church Can Help. In conjunction with the sitter service, arrange to do something relaxing and enjoyable—lunch out, shopping, or a carefully selected movie.

Legal Problems.—The uppermost concern of most parents of retarded children is, "What will happen to my retarded child when we are disabled or dead?" Most parents do not know how best to prepare a will that is "foolproof," and even a well-prepared will does not answer the concern about continuing *quality* care. That is, even if there are adequate financial resources to provide good care, how can good care be *assured*? It is not enough to seek the help of a lawyer. The lawyer needs to be knowledgeable about the field of mental retardation and the various options and alternatives for providing on-going quality care.

Many factors have to be considered:
- What is the functioning level of the retarded person?
- What is the financial situation of the family?
- Are there other family members who are willing to take over as guardians?
- Are there any quality residential facilities that are appropriate? Is there a waiting list?
- Is there someone or some organization that will serve as an advocate to make certain that maximum care and services are being provided?

There are no easy answers. Some states have more alternatives to offer regarding wills and trusts, guardianships, advocacy, residential programs, and day programs. For

information, contact your state convention office or the CPS Special Ministries Unit, Sunday School Board of the Southern Baptist Convention, Nashville, Tennessee.

↓

How the Church Can Help. Refer the family to a knowledgeable Christian attorney who can guide and advise in these critical matters.

Spiritual Problems.—Spiritual nurture is critical to the parents of mentally retarded children. Coming to terms with the presence and reality of a retarded son or daughter is vital for the spiritual welfare of the parents.

Burdens of parents are increased by false explanations and theories about the "reasons" for the existence of mental retardation. Scripture is used out of context to make devastating judgments on the parents.

Often those who seek to counsel parents avoid saying "I don't know!" Instead, they use cliches and pat statements that only add to the burden of parents. Those who counsel *must* be honest.

Parents will *never* come to terms with their retarded children without a close relationship to God.

Spiritual nurture can be developed only through the following activities:
• Bible study
• Prayer and meditation
• Fellowship with other Christians
• Actively participating in worship services

↓

How the Church Can Help. The church can:
• Encourage and lead parents in developing good spiritual nurture habits.
• Provide sitter and respite care services and other church programs for mentally retarded persons to allow the parents to attend all worship services, church programs, and other activities.
• Make it possible for parents to participate in a weekday Bible study group.

How the Church Can Minister in Tangible Ways

- Start and develop a Sunday School class for retarded persons.
- Make available an extended service for retarded persons so their parents can attend worship service. If the retarded person has appropriate behavior and can attend the worship service, he should do so. Some churches have a regular reserved place for the special education members during the worship service. This allows the class teachers to sit with them.
- Vacation Bible School is an excellent way to secure new members in Sunday School and also to secure prospective teachers.
- A sitter service is an extremely practical way to demonstrate love and concern in action. It allows the parents to be together without the pressure of looking after their retarded child.
- Respite (relief) care allows a family to take weekend trips, vacations, respond to emergencies, and other similar urgent matters. A trained sitter or sitters can provide tangible love in action.
- Church weekday activity centers can include retarded children of church members in their regular child care program. This requires cooperative staff members and parents.
- Group homes sponsored by the local church are one of the greatest needs expressed by many Christian parents. They want their adult child in a quality residential program with a committed Christian atmosphere. Several such programs are in planning stages in various states.
- Serve as an information resource to help parents secure all available and appropriate services. These services would include names of professional workers, special programs, and financial assistance.

Based upon specific needs, churches can respond in unlimited and unique ways to family needs. But the ultimate question asked by parents of retarded persons is this: "What will happen to our retarded child when we are dead?" Churches that provide answers to this question will minister to families at one of the most critical levels of concern.

Personal Learning Activities

1. List three good and three bad results which may be caused by the presence of a retarded person in the family.

2. What kinds of attitudes are exhibited by families with retarded members?

3. What is the most urgent concern felt by most families with a retarded member?

4. What is usually the first response of parents to the realization that they have a retarded child?

5. How can the church minister to parents of retarded persons?

Wholeness

God, in perfection,
Planned wholeness—
      Of body,
        And mind,
          And soul.

      Knowing that plan,
      I don't understand
      Why all of God's children
      Aren't whole.

But God, in His wisdom,
Gave me no gift
      To heal
        The body,
          The mind.

      So, I rejoice today,
      That He has trusted me
      With the gift of guiding
      The soul.

—Terry Kirkland

---

[1]From *Children's Leadership*, April 1982. © Copyright 1982 The Sunday School Board of the Southern Baptist Convention. All rights reserved. Used by permission.

Chapter 7

Curriculum

A curriculum planned around the needs of each individual class member becomes a powerful aid in teaching biblical truths. The word "Curriculum" has been given a dry, dull reputation. Far from it. The alert creative teacher recognizes the limitless opportunities for learning and takes advantage of them.

Curriculum Defined

Curriculum is anything that affects the learning process. Curriculum can be planned, or it can happen spontaneously. It can and should be enjoyable.

A curriculum is anything that helps a teacher teach and a learner learn. For example, a book can be considered curriculum. But so is a verbal affirmation, a song, a filmstrip, or a variety of other things.

Curriculum is the link between teacher and learner. All three are important.

Before learning can take place, there must be a readiness to learn.

Before teaching can take place, the teacher must be prepared to teach.

What and How Do I Teach?

"What do I teach a mentally retarded person? How do I teach a mentally retarded person?" These are the two most often asked questions by teachers and prospective teachers of mentally retarded children and adults.

There is no one answer. Just as there are many levels and personalities among retarded persons, there are also many methods of teaching biblical truths to retarded persons.

The objective is to teach persons biblical truths!

Some retarded persons can read well and comprehend even subtle messages. Others are nonreaders, and others are nonverbal (no one knows accurately what or how much is comprehended). Some learn best by listening. Others learn best by seeing. Still others learn by doing.

Rather than seeking one best way to teach, it it best to become familiar with good teaching principles.

Teachers Are Learners

The serious teacher is also a serious learner.

There are many inexpensive resources for the new or inexperienced teacher.

Recommended basic titles (available through Baptist Book Stores) include:

Preschool: *Understanding Today's Preschoolers* by Sybil Waldrop

Children: *Basic Children's Sunday School Work* by Elsie Rives; *Teaching Children in Sunday School* by Muriel Blackwell and Elsie Rives

Youth: *Basic Youth Sunday School Work* by Myrte Veach

Adult: *Basic Adult Sunday School Work* by Larry Shotwell

Although these publications are not specifically for the area of mental retardations, they are good resources for a study of teaching principles.

Reaching and Teaching Mentally Retarded Persons (now out of print, but may still be available in Baptist Book Stores and the church media library) by Doris Monroe is a good reference for workers with retarded persons of all ages.

Ministering to Persons with Mental Retardation and Their Families by Gene Nabi emphasizes the church's role with the family.

Study course credit is available for each of these books.

Many other study course books for general and specific areas of interest may be relevant on an individual basis. A list is available through the local church office. (See a *Baptist Book Store Catalog.*)

In addition, the new or inexperienced worker will benefit from studying one or more of the resource kits for the different age groups. Recommended kits include these:

Resource Kit for Bible Searchers (ages 10-11)
Resource Kit for Bible Discoverers (ages 8-9)
Resource Kit for Bible Learners (ages 6-7)
Children's Bible Study Resource Kit (ages 6-11)
Bible Story Time at Church Resource Kit (birth-5)

These kits contain a variety of excellent teaching aids and instructions. These kits can be secured through the local church office on the Church Literature Order form.

Book knowledge, of course, is not enough. Good teachers are people-oriented and have characteristics that makes the task of teaching a joyful challenge!

With mentally retarded persons, a planned curriculum is especially important. A planned curriculum should: one, have a clear and practical goal; two, be sequential and orderly; three, be individualized; and four, involve the learner.

Available Resources

Special Ministries Resource Kit—Sunday School/Church Training—
This quarterly kit, formerly titled *Sunday School Resource Kit for Teaching the Mentally Retarded*, is available for use with persons with various disabilities—including mental retardation, deafness, learning disabilities, and various multiple handicaps. Although the kit has been developed on a "basic" and "advanced" level, it can be adapted to many mental levels. Generally, the "basic" level is recommended for persons who have great difficulty in reading or cannot read; the "advanced" level is recommended for persons who can read or are higher functioning.

The kit is based on the Convention Uniform Series themes and lessons. It contains the following elements:

• Teacher's Guide (two copies)
• Suggested Guidelines for Teachers of Deaf Children
• Suggested Guidelines for Teachers of Mentally Retarded Persons
• Resources for each level, basic and advanced
• Six bold, four-color teaching pictures
• Nineteen teaching activities

The teacher's guide is prepared for working with two levels: basic and advanced. Although there are no distinct guidelines for what level is most suitable for what group, a general guideline is that the basic is for younger and nonreading persons and that the advanced is for more mature and reading persons. With adaptation, both levels can be used for either group.

The kit can be used for both Sunday School and Church Training by alternating between the levels. For example, use the advanced level for Sunday School and the basic level for Church Training.

Because the kit is based on the Convention Uniform Series, other materials in this series can be used to supplement the weekly program, depending on the needs of the group. If the kit is not challenging enough, then other Convention Uniform Series materials can be used because they carry the same unit theme and lesson topics.

Example:

The special education class is made up mostly of adults who can read on at least a third-grade level. These persons may want to use the periodical *Sunday School Lessons—Special Ministries* to supplement the material in the kit.

Example:

The special education class is made up of teenagers who can only recognize the most simple words and who are less mature. With this group, the *Children's Bible Study* may be more appropriate. The variations are almost limitless.

If one series is not suitable, the teacher should try another until the right combinations are found.

It is recommended that the *Special Ministries Resources Kit— Sunday School/Church Training* be used as the base teaching component. For special situations, contact the Special Ministries Unit, Sunday School Board.

Titles and levels of the Convention Uniform Series include the following:

Title	Intended For
Sunday School Lessons—Special Ministries	Adults who can read at about 2.5 to 3.0 level
Children's Bible Study—Older Pupil	Age level 9-11
Children's Bible Study—Younger Pupil	Age level 6-8
Bible Story Time at Home	Age 3-5
Bible Stories for Me	Birth-2

All of these materials are listed on the Church Literature Dated Form under Convention Uniform Series.

Church Training

Although at present there are no specific Church Training materials for use with mentally retarded persons, any of the previously cited titles can be used *with adaptation*. Also, the Church Training curriculum *Exploring* 2 (ages 9-11) and *Exploring* 1 (ages 6-8) may be appropriate for adapting to the levels of your class members.

Every church that has a special education department in the Sunday School should have a corresponding Church Training group. A special Church Training program allows the church to minister to the full family during Church Training time.

Where there is no Sunday School program for retarded persons, a Church Training program may be the first step in developing a comprehensive ministry to mentally retarded persons and their families.

Again with adaptation, it is possible that church Training age-group materials can be used for program topics, outlines, and content.

It is best not to use the same teachers for both the Sunday School and Church Training programs.

Extended Session

For churches committed to offering a full ministry to mentally retarded persons and their families, extended sessions should be included. An extended session is conducted during the same time as the morning or evening worship service. This allows other family members to attend the worship services.

Too often, because there is no program available for the retarded member of the family, the full family cannot or does not attend either or both worship services.

For persons of younger ages, the *Extended Session for 4's and 5's* packet can be used for extended sessions. This packet includes a special section on how to adapt the material for retarded persons.

For those of older ages, the *Children's Worship Resource Kit* can

be used at either extended session. This kit can be adapted according to the ability level of the group members.

Midweek Service

A program can be adapted or created for retarded persons during the midweek service or prayer meeting so that the full family can attend the midweek service.

This session need not be so formally structured as the other programs and may consist more of music, recreational activities, Bible stories, and other related activities.

Program ideas may be adapted from any of the preceding materials.

Vacation Bible School

The VBS *Resource Kit for Younger Children* (ages 6-7) can be adapted without difficulty for use with retarded persons. The Special Ministries Unit of the Sunday School Board makes available a set of recommended adaptations of this VBS kit for use with retarded persons. These are available through the state Sunday School convention office and the associational office.

Good Teaching Requires Planning

Teaching techniques and methods are limitless. But whatever the approach, planning and preparation are required. A session planning sheet is useful in developing a good program. A suggested completed format is shown on page 91.

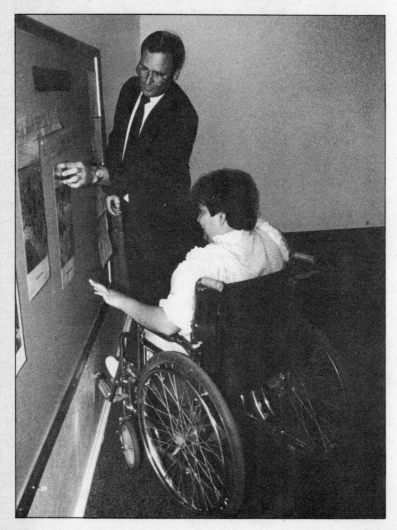

SESSION PLANNING SHEET

UNIT TITLE Getting along with others

DESIRED OUTCOME God wants me to be a good helper

UNIT OBJECTIVES to share materials & center activities; to learn ways to help others

SESSION 2 (Date September 9, 1984)

Session Emphasis God wants me to be a good neighbor

Special Bible Verse Love your neighbor as yourself (Romans 13:9)

Activities	Supplies Needed	Person Responsible
Bible Story Pillows	Fabric, Crayons, Muslin Filler	Charlotte
Ink Printing	ink brayer, ink, construction paper, meat trays	Mamye
Bible Verse Folder	construction paper, crayons	Delores

Bible Story The Good Samaritan **Reference**: Luke 10:25-37

Songs-Titles | **Song Location**

*God Wants Us to Be Kind	More Songs for 4's & 5's p.21
Jesus Loves Me	Baptist Hymnal p. 336
God is So Good	Hap Palmer's Record

Kit Items Needed
Item #19 -- Teaching Picture   Item #38 Community Helpers
*Item #32 -- Unit Song

Special Preparations	Person Responsible
Filmstrip FS 435 - Community Helpers	Mayme
Popcorn	Charlotte
Color Mobile	Delores

The Key Is to Adapt

No two retarded persons are exactly alike. Hence, no one teaching approach or one set of curriculum materials will meet all the learning needs of a retarded person. Quality teaching requires *adapting* to meet the needs of retarded persons.

Retarded persons learn through *all* the senses: sight, sound, touch, smell, and taste. Just as with other persons, each retarded person learns best through one or two of the senses. Generally, most retarded persons learn best through sight and sound.

So if the material you use as part of the curriculum seems too "childish" or too adult, then adapt the material to meet the needs of your group. Often a slight change will make a great difference. Additional pictures, relevant stories, or a new twist to a game or activity can create greater interest and learning.

The committed, creative teacher will explore, experiment, and adapt to find the materials that will best help teach biblical truths.

Special Problems

All teaching situations have special problems or challenges because all individual class members and teachers are different personalities. Described here are four examples of more common problems that are found in the special education department:
- Mainstreaming Versus Separate Department
- Medical (Seizures)
- Behavior Management
- Nutrition

Mainstreaming Versus Separate Department

"Mainstreaming" is the contemporary term for the effort to integrate exceptional individuals into schools, residential facilities, and other service systems commonly available to the "normal" members of the community.

The ideal objective in church programming is to "mainstream," or to place retarded persons in programs with their age peers. But this requires three prerequisites:

- The retarded person should not have any extreme behavior problems that would disrupt other class members.
- The teacher should be knowledgeable about the problem of mental retardation and should have a commitment to work with retarded persons.
- The other students should be aware and accepting of the retarded person. Most students will adopt the behavior and attitude of the teacher.

However, if there are inappropriate and disruptive behaviors or if the retarded person cannot benefit from being mainstreamed, then a separate department is appropriate.

If a student is mainstreamed, it may be beneficial to provide the student or students with a teacher who would concentrate on the retarded person.

Seizures

About 20 percent of persons with mental retardation have a specific diagnosis and receive medical treatment. The problem of seizures among this group is not uncommon.

Probably the reason many persons do not wish to become involved in the area of mental retardation is because of their fear of being responsible for a person who suddenly has a seizure. These attacks (losses of consciousness) may be extremely brief or rare.

Medications are effective in controlling seizures, so the incidence of seizures is much reduced. But still the thought of someone under your care having a seizure can be unnerving.

With instructions from parents or the responsible person, the problem of epilepsy can be minimized.

Such information about epilepsy and other medical problems ought to be fully documented in the Individual Information Sheet included in Chapter 4.

Behavior Management

It is not uncommon for groups of retarded children and adults to be well behaved and without disruptive actions. More often than not, retarded persons are a pleasure and are responsive to the teacher.

But there are incidents of inappropriate behavior from time to time, and discipline and structure are required in the classroom.

The alert, observing teacher can identify the *reasons* for inappropriate behavior by noting what takes place just before and immediately after the inappropriate behavior.

A general working principle is:

Ignore inappropriate behavior, and

Reward appropriate behavior.

No one method always works with certain inappropriate behaviors. Good teachers are always increasing their knowledge and skills at behavior management.

A good resource is *Behavior Problems* by Bruce Baker, Allen Brightman, Louis Heifetz, and Diane Murphy (Research Press).

Even moderately or severely retarded persons can learn what is acceptable behavior. Sometimes removal from the room or group is necessary. For continued inappropriate or disruptive actions, the best reaction is to not allow the person to be with the group for one or more weeks. This is a last resort, of course; but it may be the only one that works. No one should ever be degraded, insulted, or embarrassed because of his behavior. Persons with mental retardation have the same needs and sensitivities as other persons and respond best to love and discipline.

Nutrition

A great deal of information has been gathered and reported about the effects of nutrition on mental development and physical well being. The effects of alcohol and drugs are well known. However, mental and physical welfare can be negatively affected by certain foods: granulated sugar, food coloring, white flour, and others.

Snacks should be carefully selected. "Junk" foods should be avoided.

Fresh fruit, fruit juices, peanut butter, and dairy products offer a more healthy snack. Ask about allergies or food dislikes and include this on the Individual Information Sheet in Chapter 4.

Personal Learning Activities

1. Define curriculum.
2. What is the objective in teaching retarded person?
3. The serious teacher is also a serious _____.
4. A planned curriculum should
   (1)
   (2)
   (3)
   (4)
5. Because no two retarded persons are exactly alike, the key in teaching is to _____.

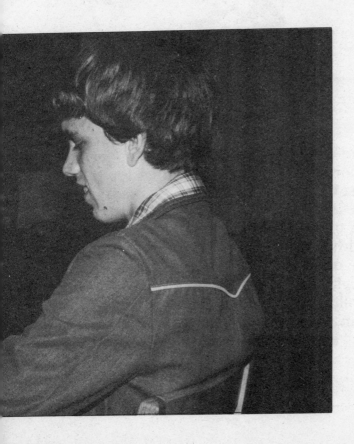

The time of accountability is the moment of grace when one is brought to a decision for or against Christ by the Spirit. This moment requires the proclamation of the Word, the drawing of the Spirit, and the yielding of the individual to God. Until this moment is possible, one may leave children in the hands of God. Evidences are that we are holding very young children accountable for too much and not holding adults, who have professed Christ, accountable for enough.[1]

---

[1]William L. Hendricks, A *Theology for Children* (Nashville: Broadman Press, 1980), p. 251.

Chapter 8

Mental Retardation and Conversion

Conversion can be experienced by many mentally retarded persons!

This fact is ignored by many Christians who believe that because a person is labeled "mentally retarded," that in itself assures automatic entry into the kingdom of God. This relieves the Christian teacher, pastor, and friend of the responsibility to present the message of salvation in clear and simple terms. As with young children, leading retarded persons to make professions of faith is easy. To do this without regard for the validity of the profession of faith would be irresponsible. Using this as an excuse, however, not to witness at all is also irresponsible.

Two Points of View

Pastor A: *Certainly I believe that anyone can make a public profession of faith; that is, if that person fully understands what he is doing. This means that the convert understands that he is a sinner and repents and accepts Jesus Christ as Lord and Savior and promises to live according to the commands of Jesus.*

I doubt that a mentally retarded person has this level of understanding. So I would only counsel with a retarded person. God has provided for them, anyway.

Pastor B: *I don't have the ability to judge which persons are making a valid public profession of faith. If a mentally retarded person* *wishes to accept Jesus as Savior, I am obligated to accept that person, with counseling, which allows me to further explain the meaning of the gospel in simple, clear terms. I should do the same for anyone. I leave the judging up to God.*

Mental retardation and conversion cannot be adequately covered in the most detailed systematic theology, much less in the next few pages. The emphasis of this chapter is to urge persons to see retarded persons as *spiritual* beings. Seeing them in this way will change our attitudes, beliefs, and behavior as we work with retarded persons.

If we do not see them as spiritual beings—as persons in development—then we imply that retarded persons are incapable of responding to God's love, and we become judges of God's creation.

But there is a case for both points of view. Retarded persons—just as normal persons—learn through watching and mimicking. Now, consider what they see when someone responds to the invitation and makes a public profession of faith: A person walks down the aisle. He is greeted by the pastor who shakes the person's hand and may even put an arm around the person's shoulder. The person is introduced to the congregation in a positive way. The person is officially accepted by the whole congregation as they all raise their hands. After the benediction, the person is welcomed into the fellowship by many of the congregation as they shake hands, hug, and say positive statements. The person may even have his picture taken!

So, to some retarded persons, the invitation may be a pleasant social experience without any understanding of the conversion experience.

But, for many retarded persons, there can be an understanding of what it means to become a Christian. Just as many "normal" children are accepted into the Christian faith at younger ages, many retarded persons have the ability to understand the theological basics of becoming a Christian: sin, repentance, salvation, commitment.

The awesome responsibility of the teacher and pastor is to

explain to the retarded person who has expressed an interest in becoming a Christian how to do so. This explanation must be done in simple, clear, concrete terms—the *same* way it should be explained to anyone!

Crystal Clear Clarification

Just as with anyone, terms ought to be used that are clear and understood by the class member. For example, don't say "Be reverent in church." Say "Pay attention," or "Be quiet and listen." If the religious term cannot be explained simply and clearly, then it should not be used!

The Christian faith has countless theological and religious terms that are used, but these terms have different meanings for different people. For example:

Heaven	**Grace**	**Messiah**
Hell	**Evil**	**Savior**
Sin	**Mercy**	**Atonement**
Repentance	**Lord**	**Faith**
Salvation	**King**	**Spirit**

These terms, at best, are difficult to explain in simple, clear language. These and other such terms should be avoided. Instead, the language that the retarded person understands should be used.

Not: "Let's all be reverent in church today."

But: "Let's all pay attention, sit still, and be quiet in church today."

Lost, Saved, Safe

The spiritual status of a mentally retarded person has been the topic of much debate. Attitudes vary to extremes, as shown by the two pastors at the beginning of this chapter.

Mentally retarded persons have often been described as

children in their level of comprehension. Jesus had powerful statements about children and their relationship to God.

> Mark 10:13-16: "And they brought young children to him, that he should touch them: and his disciples rebuked those that brought them. But when Jesus saw it, he was much displeased, and said unto them, Suffer the little children to come unto me, and forbid them not: for of such is the kingdom of God. Verily I say unto you, Whosoever shall not receive the kingdom of God as a little child, he shall not enter therein. And he took them up in his arms, put his hands upon them, and blessed them."

Mentally retarded persons can be categorized in three spiritual groups, just as can anyone else:

Lost.—Those who have the capability to understand what it means to become a Christian but have not been taught or have not responded to the message of the gospel are lost. They need the gospel message.

Mark 16:15: "And he said unto them, Go ye into all the world,
and preach the gospel to every creature."

Saved.—Those who have the capability to understand what it means to become a Christian and have been taught and have made a profession of faith.

Safe.—Persons who are profoundly retarded and have extremely low levels of comprehension are safe within God's saving grace. While the fact of salvation is a mystery in itself, what we do know about God is sufficient to know that His love encompasses those of a "childlike" nature.

Mark 9:36-37: "And he took a child, and set him in the midst of
them: and when he had taken him in his arms,
he said unto them, Whosoever shall receive one of such children
in my name, receiveth me: and whosoever shall receive me,
receiveth not me, but him that sent me."

> Mark 9:42: "And whosoever shall offend one of these little ones that believe in me, it is better for him that a millstone were hanged about his neck, and he were cast into the sea."

With persons of this spiritual nature, the Christian has the responsibility to demonstrate God's love, God's love is expressed through the Christian teacher, parent, friend, and pastor by words, tones, attitudes of acceptance, empathy, and care.

How to Minister

How does one minister to a mentally retarded person regarding conversion? Just as one would minister to any other person.

Become acquainted with the retarded person. Come to see that person as a human being with the same needs as other human beings. Develop a friendship. Learn about that person's background, likes, dislikes, level of mental ability, and other information that will help you establish a strong fellowship bond.

Make spiritual matters a natural part of your conversations. Use terms that are clear, concrete, and simple. This ministry will require prayer and preparation.

Do not use pressure. Most retarded persons are easily led by persons they like and trust.

If the person expresses an interest in making a profession of faith, arrange for a counseling session with the pastor. The retarded person may want someone to accompany him to this session.

Once the pastor is satisfied that the decision is valid, then the pastor, teacher, and family should make plans for a public profession.

The pastor should be educated about mental retardation. A sensitive pastor can lead the congregation into an exciting ministry with mentally retarded persons and their families.

MYTHS AND FACTS

Myth: A mentally retarded adult really has the mind of a child.
Fact: In some ways, he does; but many retarded adults have adult interests.

Myth: A mentally retarded person has limited spiritual understanding.
Fact: A mentally retarded person accepts great spiritual truths without question: God loves me; the Golden Rule; the Ten Commandments, and others.

Myth: It takes a great deal of patience and love to teach retarded persons.
Fact: No more than it does to work with "normal" adolescents or teenagers!

Myth: Mentally retarded persons are not accountable for themselves spiritually or morally.
Fact: They are if they comprehend the gospel message.

Myth: Mentally retarded persons really have poor memory and learn only through many repetitions.
Fact: Many retarded persons have highly gifted memory skills.

Personal Learning Activities

1. What are the three spiritual categories of retarded persons?

2. How does one minister to a mentally retarded person regarding conversion?

3. When speaking to retarded persons about spiritual matters, you should use terms that are _____, _____, and _____.

4. List at least one myth you have heard about mentally retarded persons.

What is amazing about the findings and predictions of the contributing authors of this book is their claim that the goal of "cure" of mental retardation is not only possible, but possible in many areas within our lifetime. . . . As the data converge from such diverse scientific disciplines as neuropathology, behavioral science, biochemistry, psychiatry, neurosurgery, genetics, and endocrinology, they indicate—in overwhelming fashion—that we are on the brink of startling break-throughs that can lead us to "curing" many of our current and future mentally retarded citizens.[1]

[1] Frank J. Menolascino, Ronald Neman, and Jack A. Stark, *Curative Aspects of Mental Retardation: Biomedical and Behavioral Advances* (Baltimore: P. H. Brookes Publishing Co. 1983), pp. 301-302.

Chapter 9

New Hope

What Message from the Church?

The Christian's life is based on hope. Even in the midst of tragedy, the early church suddenly mushroomed because of the experience of a new hope: the resurrection of Jesus. Out of disaster, pain, and grief, there came new hope.

What about the problem of mental retardation? Can there be new hope? For parents and families of mentally retarded persons—especially those who are severely and profoundly affected—rarely is there hope for a "normal" life for either the retarded person or for the family.

There is a wide range of parental hopes regarding retarded children:

> "I prayed and prayed and prayed for my mentally retarded son to be healed, believing the Scripture about the unlimited power of prayer. My son is twenty-four and still retarded. Maybe the power of prayer is limited. Maybe God did not hear me. Then, again, maybe God did."—
> A Father

> "I just pray that my retarded daughter will be happy. That is all."—
> A Mother

The great majority of parents, family members, and teachers of retarded persons do not entertain the possibility of a reversal of the symptoms of mental retardation. A sobering sense of realism is evident when one works with a retarded person. Even the cute antics of a retarded child become embarrassing as the child becomes an adult and continues to exhibit childish, immature, and inappropriate behavior.

So to most people mental retardation represents ultimate hopelessness.

What Message from the Bible?

The term "mental retardation" is relatively recent, being preceded by many negative labels (some are valid medical terms):

Moron (moderately retarded person)
Imbecile (severely retarded person)
Idiot (profoundly retarded person)
Feebleminded (all retarded persons)
Mongoloid idiot (profoundly retarded Down's Syndrome)

New Testament writers used various terms to describe the behavior of those who might have been categorized as mentally retarded and multiple handicapped persons. For example:

> "Then was brought unto him one possessed with a devil, blind, and dumb: and he healed him, insomuch that the blind and dumb both spoke and saw" (Matt. 12:22).

> "And in that same hour he cured many of their infirmities and plagues, and of evil spirits; and unto many that were blind he gave sight" (Luke 7:21).

These two passages could have been referring to some of the characteristics of mental retardation. The term "mentally retarded" did not come into use until the 1950s.

But the overriding message of the Scripture is that the needs of *any* handicapped person demand our response and ministry.

Is There Hope in Prevention and Treatment?

Yes!

If what has been learned about prevention and treatment in the field of mental retardation were actually implemented, the incidence of retardation would be reduced by at least 75 percent!

Eleven recommendations have been made by the President's Committee on Mental Retardation and include:
• Public education
• Research
• Health delivery systems
• Nutrition
• Immunization
• Family planning
• Programs for pregnant teenagers
• Prenatal care
• Newborn screening
• Caring for immature infants
• Early childhood education and intervention

There are many opportunities for concerned Christians to become involved in supportive ways in these areas.

Is There Hope for a Cure?

Physicians, professional workers, and parents have avoided using the term "cure" with reference to retardation for three reasons:
• Little or no evidence exists to support any such happening.
• Genetic and hereditary causes have always been considered permanent.
• To create false hope in parents and other family members would be cruel.

Perhaps the problem is twofold: (1) The meaning of the word "cure" and (2) how severe the problem is. For example, just as an amputated limb cannot be regrown a profoundly retarded and multiple handicapped person cannot have the characteristics removed.

But according to Frank K. Menolascino, psychiatrist and former president of the National Association for Retarded Citizens, if we define "cure" as a significant increase in the level of intellectual functioning and social adaptation, there is hope!

In 1980, the Association for Retarded Citizens—U.S. (formerly known as the National Association for Retarded Citizens) held a conference entitled: "Mental Retardation: The Search for Cures."

An increasing body of research results provides evidence that there is hope with reference to the curative aspects of mental retardation.

It is time for the appropriate use of this word. Furthermore, the church has a responsibility in introducing an attitude of hope about the problem. Christians should not say simply that "improvement" is possible. Perhaps our restrictive attitudes place obstacles in the healing aspects of God's power.

Certainly many profoundly hurt persons are multiple handicapped with the most severe limitations. To suggest that these persons can become "normal" would be glib. But it would be spiritually irresponsible for mature Christians to have the same attitude of hopelessness for the 89 percent of all retarded persons—those labeled "mildly retarded"—when there is no definitive cause.

What, then, are we to do?

We are to do as the Master directed: Pray without ceasing. We are to pray specifically, expectantly, thankfully, compassionately, and continually.

We are not to pray as one who has tried everything else first, but as one who prays *first* and waits for God's leading.

The message of the church has not changed: God's redemptive grace provides salvation for man's sinful and rebellious nature. This message is intended for everyone, including parents of retarded persons. But the daily worry, frustration, pain, and grief have occupied the attention of parents to the exclusion of the real hope.

The task of each Christian is to minister to both the retarded person and his family.

Personal Learning Activities

1. Of the eleven recommendations made by the President's Committee on Mental Retardation, which do you believe are the three most important? Why?
2. What is the message of the church?
3. What is the hope of the Christian based on?

GOD'S WILL

Many Christians believe that mental retardation is an act of God as punishment or as a method of teaching a person to become more caring.
Some people believe that God seeks out a particular family in which to entrust the care of a retarded person.
These persons consider mental retardation to be the will of God.
God is a God of love, and to consider God in any other image other than a loving Father would be spiritually misleading.
God does not inflict punishment on a grandchild to teach the grandparent a lesson.
God does not make a child profoundly retarded to bring the parents closer to God.
Rather, the presence of a retarded person in the family can be a spiritually deepening experience because of the family's response.
Most parents and family members would never want to unlearn what they have learned because of the retarded person.
One parent said: "Having a retarded child is a high price to pay, but the cost does not even approach the value received."

Chapter 10

Finally . . .

The prospects for mentally retarded persons and their families are exciting!

Christians are beginning to recognize the needs and abilities of retarded persons.

The church has limitless possibilities for ministering to millions of persons whose hurt and inner pain will respond only to the healing message of the gospel.

Mental retardation is a problem of almost overwhelming dimensions. It requires an organized response with God's overwhelming love and power.

Many practical ways help God's redemption and healing take place:

1. If your church has no Sunday School class for retarded persons, be a catalyst in starting one.

2. If your church already has a Sunday School class for retarded persons, be a catalyst in expanding this ministry to include a—

• Morning extended session to allow parents and family to attend the worship service.
• Program during the Church Training period.
• Summer activity program.
• Sitter and respite care program.
• Group home.
• Sheltered workshop program.

3. Encourage church members to learn about the ministry of mental retardation by attending special sessions at each of the Sunday School leadership weeks during the summer at the Glorieta (New Mexico) and Ridgecrest (North Carolina) Baptist Conference Centers.

Other training opportunities are often available during other weeks at the Conference Centers: Vacation Bible School Institutes; Large Sunday School Week; and, from time to time, Small Sunday School Week and Church Training Week.

Not every associational or state convention office has an active program in the area of mental retardation. Work through your church to urge that mental retardation be included as a priority.

There are a few excellent programs at the associational level. For example, Liberty Baptist Association in Arkansas holds a retreat for retarded persons and their parents and teachers.

Several state convention offices work actively in conducting statewide retreats and training programs: Florida, Alabama, Louisiana, Tennessee, South Carolina, Virginia, California, Texas, and Mississippi.

Ridgecrest

One state convention—Georgia—is conducting a group home ministry. The Tennessee Baptist Children's Home has on its campus a respite care facility for mentally retarded children. Other states are planning or preparing to begin such a ministry.

The most urgent need of families with a retarded member is expressed in the universal quest on the lips and in the hearts of parents and other family members: "What will happen to our retarded child when we die?" The best answer can come only from the church.

Glorieta

Appendix A: *Organizations and Agencies As Resources*

An increasing number of private organizations can provide general information and specfic help. The following is a brief list. Addresses change, so you may wish to confirm the correct address by contacting your local public library. A full list of organizations dedicated to the various handicapping conditions can be found in *Encyclopedia of Associations*, 1985, 19th Edition, Volume 1 (Parts 1 and 2), *National Organizations of the* U.S., published by Gale Research Company, Book Tower, Detroit, MI 48226:

American Association on Mental Deficiency, 1719 Kalorama Road, Washington, DC 20009.

American Foundation for the Blind, 15 West 16th Street, New York, NY 10011

American Printing House for the Blind, 1839 Frankfort, P. O. Box 6085, Louisville, KY 40206.

American Speech-Language-Hearing Association, 10801 Rockville Pike, Rockville, MD 20852

Association for Children and Adults with Learning Disabilities, 4156 Library Road, Pittsburgh, PA 15234

Association for Retarded Citizens—U.S., P. O. Box 6109, Arlington, TX 76011

The Association for the Severely Handicapped, 7010 Roosevelt, NE, Seattle, WA 98115

Boy Scouts of America, Scouting for the Handicapped Division, Boy Scouts of America, North Brunswick, NJ 08902

Council for Exceptional Children, 1920 Association Drive, Reston, VA 22091

Epilepsy Foundation of America, 4351 Garden City Drive, Landover, MD 20785

Girl Scouts of the U.S.A., Scouting for Handicapped Girls Program, 830 Third Avenue, New York, NY 10022

The Joseph P. Kennedy, Jr. Foundation, Special Olympics, 1701 K Street, NW, Suite 205, Washington, DC 20006

March of Dimes Birth Defects Foundation, 1275 Mamaroneck Avenue, White Plains, NY 10605

National Mental Health Association, 1201 Prince Street, Arlington, VA 22314

National Association for Music Therapy, 1133 15th Street, NW, Washington, DC 20005

National Down's Syndrome Congress, 1640 W. Roosevelt Road, Chicago, IL 60608

National Easter Seal Society, 2023 W. Ogden Avenue, Chicago, IL 60612

National Information Center for Handicapped Children and Youth, Closer Look, Box 1492, Washington, DC 20013

The National Society for Children and Adults with Autism, 1234 Massachusett Avenue, NW, Sta. 1017, Washington, DC 20005

United Cerebral Palsy Associations, 66 East 34th Street, New York, NY 10016

National Agencies

The President's Committee on Employment of the Handicapped, Washington, DC 20210

The President's Committee on Mental Retardation, Washington, DC 20201

The Superintendent of Documents, U.S. Government Printing Office, Washington, DC 20402

Appendix B: State Convention Resources

For information about mental retardation ministries in your state, contact each State Convention:

ALABAMA—205/288-2460
2001 E. South Boulevard
P. O. Box 11870
Montgomery, AL 36198

ALASKA—907/344-9627
1750 O'Malley Rd.
Anchorage, AK 99516

ARIZONA—602/264-9421
Suite 102
400 W. Camelback Road
Phoenix, AZ 85013

ARKANSAS—501/376-4791
Room 206
525 W. Capitol Avenue (72201)
P. O. Box 552
Little Rock, AR 72203

CALIFORNIA—209/229-9533
678 E. Shaw Avenue (93710)
P. O. Box 5168
Fresno, CA 93755

COLORADO—303/771-2480
7393 S. Alton Way
Englewood, Colorado (80112)
P. O. Box 22005
Denver, CO 80222

DISTRICT OF COLUMBIA—
202/265-1526
1628 Sixteenth Street
Washington, DC 20009

FLORIDA—904/396-2351
Florida Baptist Building
1230 Hendricks Avenue
Jacksonville, FL 32207

GEORGIA—404/455-0404
Baptist Center
2930 Flowers Road, S.
Atlanta, GA 30341

HAWAII—808/946-9581
Hawaii Baptist Convention
2042 Vancouver Drive
Honolulu, HI 96822

ILLINOIS—217/876-2639
3085 E. Adlai
   Stevenson Drive (62703)
P. O. Box 3486
Springfield, IL 62708

INDIANA—317/241-9317
900 N. High School Road
P. O. Box 24189
Indianapolis, IN 46224

IOWA—515/278-1566
2400 86th Street, Suite 27
Des Moines, IA 50322

KANSAS-NEBRASKA—913/273-4880
5410 W. Seventh
Topeka, KS 66606

KENTUCKY—502/245-4101
10701 Shelbyville Road
P. O. Box 43433
Middletown, KY 40243

LOUISIANA—318/448-3402
1250 MacArthur Drive
Box 311
Alexandria, LA 71309

MARYLAND—301/321-7900
1313 York Road, Baptist Building
Lutherville, MD 21093

MICHIGAN—313/557-4200
15635 W. Twelve Mile Road
Southfield, MI 48076

MINNESOTA/WISCONSIN—
507/282-3636
519 Sixteenth Street, SE
Rochester, MN 55904

MISSISSIPPI—601/968-3800
515 Mississippi Street (39201)
P. O. Box 530
Jackson, MS 39205

MISSOURI—314/635-7931
Missouri Baptist Building
400 E. High Street
Jefferson City, MO 65101

NEVADA—702/786-0406
P. O. Box 6538
Reno, NE (89513)
406 California Ave.
Reno, NV 89509

NEW ENGLAND—617/393-6013
5 Oak Avenue
P. O. Box 688
Northborough, MA 01532-0688

NEW MEXICO—505/247-0586
616 Central Avenue, SE
P. O. Box 485
Albuquerque, NM 87103

NEW YORK—315/475-6173
Suite 934
500 S. Salina Street
Syracuse, NY 13202

NORTH CAROLINA—
919/467-5100
205 Convention Drive
Cary, North Carolina 27611
P. O. Box 26508
Raleigh, NC 27611

NORTHERN PLAINS—
605/343-5572
924 Quincy
P. O. Box 1278
Rapid City, SD 57709

NORTHWEST—503/238-4545
1033 NE Sixth Avenue
Portland, OR 97232

OHIO—614/258-8491
1680 E. Broad Street
Columbus, OH 43203

OKLAHOMA—405/236-4341
1141 N. Robinson Street
Oklahoma City, OK 73103

PENNSYLVANIA/SOUTH JERSEY—
717/652-5856
4620 Fritchey Street
Harrisburg, PA 17109

PUERTO RICO—809/765-7878
Detroit #10
Urb, Belisa
Rio Piedras, Puerto Rico 00926

SOUTH CAROLINA—
803/765-0030
907 Richland Street
Columbia, SC 29201

TENNESSEE—615/373-2255
107 Franklin Pike
P. O. Box 347
Brentwood, TN 37027

TEXAS—214/720-0550
Baptist General Convention
    of Texas
Sunday School Division
1104 Baptist Building, 511 N. Akard
Dallas, TX 75201

UTAH-IDAHO—
801/255-3565
P. O. Box 1039
Sandy, UT 84091

VIRGINIA—804/282-9751
5101 Monument Avenue (23230)
P. O. Box 8568
Richmond, VA 23226

WEST VIRGINIA—
304/727-2974
801 Sixth Avenue
St. Albans, WV 25177

WYOMING—307/472-4087
4270 Poison Spider Road (82604)
P. O. Box 3074
Casper, WY 82602

120

Appendix C: References Recommended for Church Media Library

These are excellent books for laypersons to get a good overview about mental retardation.

1. Allen, David F. & Victoria S., *Ethical Issues in Mental Retardation—Tragic Choices/Living Hope*. Nashville: Abingdon Press, 1979.
2. Crim, Lottie, *Come Care with Me*. Nashville: Broadman Press, 1983.
3. Dougan, Terrell; Isbell, Lyn; and Vyas, Patricia, compilers, *We Have Been There*. Nashville: Abingdon Press, 1983.
4. Perske, Robert, *Hope for the Families—New Directions for Parents of Persons with Retardation or Other Disabilities*. Nashville: Abingdon Press, 1981.
5. Perske, Robert, *New Life in the Neighborhood—How Persons with Retardation or Other Disabilities Can Help Make a Good Community Better*. Nashville: Abingdon Press, 1981.
6. Price, Eugenia, *No Pat Answers*. Grand Rapids: Zondervan Books, 1972.
7. Welborn, Terry M. and Williams, Stanley. *Leading the Mentally Retarded in Worship*. St. Louis: Concordia, 1973.

These are more technical books that may be of interest to the person who wants to learn more scientific, medical, and historical information about the problem of mental retardation.

1. Grossman, Herbert J., ed., *Classification in Mental Retardation*. Washington, D.C.: American Association on Mental Deficiency, 1977.
2. Krishef, Curtis H., *An Introduction to Mental Retardation*. Springfield, IL: Charles C. Thomas, 1983.
3. Menolascino, Frank J.; Neman, Ronald; and Stark, Jack A., *Curative Aspects of Mental Retardation*. Baltimore: P. H. Brookes Publishing Co., 1983.
4. Richmond, Julius B.; Tarjan, George; and Mendelsohn, Robert, eds., *Mental Retardation—A Handbook for the Primary Physician*. Chicago: American Medical Association, 3rd ed., 1976.
5. Scheerenberger, R. C., *A History of Mental Retardation*. Baltimore: P. H. Brookes Publishing Co., 1983.

Appendix D: Sunday School Leadership Diploma in Special Ministries—Mentally Retarded

___ 1. Basic Sunday School Work, Harry M. Piland (5163-80) or The Small Sunday School at Work, Daryl Heath, compiler (5163-03).
___ 2. Basic Children's Sunday School Work, Elsie Rives (5163–92).
___ 3. Ministering to Persons with Mental Retardation and Their Families, Gene Nabi (5161-15) or Reaching and Teaching Mentally Retarded Persons, Doris Monroe (5163-41), eligible for credit until October 1987.
___ 4. Teaching Children in Sunday School, Muriel Blackwell and Elsie Rives (5163–28).
___ 5. An Introduction to the Bible, L. D. Johnson (5132-01) or Book Alive! John W. Tresch, Jr. and Kathryn Griffin (5132–91).
___ 6. The Baptist Faith and Message, Herschel Hobbs (5133–02).

Sunday School Advanced Leadership Diploma in Special Ministries—Mental Retardation

___ 1. How to Study the Bible, Olin T. Binkley (5132-02) or How to Study Your Bible (Ec Module).
___ 2. Come Care with Me, Lottie R. Crim (Broadman 4254-31).
___ 3. Witness to Win, Max Caldwell (5130-51) or Every Christian's Job, C. E. Matthews (5130-64) or How to Witness (Ec Module).
___ 4. Jesus the Teacher, J. M. Price (5163-02) or How to Guide Preschoolers, Jenell Strickland (5161-68) or How to Guide Children, Louise Caldwell (5161-69).
___ 5. Elective from "The Christian Family" subject area.
___ 6. Advanced Leader Training Conference.
___ 7. January Bible Study Book (adult or youth) or elective from "The Bible Studies" subject area.
___ 8. Baptist Doctrine Study Book (adult or youth) or elective from the "Baptist Doctrine" subject area.

Appendix E: The Church Study Course

The Church Study Course is a Southern Baptist education system consisting of short courses for adults and youth combined with a credit and recognition system. Also available in the system are noncredit short courses (called foundational units) for children and preschoolers. The courses in the Church Study Course are for use in addition to the ongoing study and training curricula made available to churches by the denomination.

More than 500 courses are available in 23 subject areas. Courses are flexible enough to offer credit for either individual or group study. Credit is awarded for each course completed. These credits may be applied to one or more of the 100 plus diploma plans in the system. Diplomas are available for most leadership positions as well as general diplomas for all Christians. These diplomas are the certification that a person has completed from 5 to 8 prescribed courses. Diploma requirements are given in the catalogs.

"Enrollment" in a diploma plan is made by completing Form 725 "Church Study Course Enrollment/Credit Request" and sending it to the Awards Office at the Sunday School Board. Course credit may also be requested on this form. A permanent record of courses and diplomas will be maintained by the Awards Office. Twice each year up-to-date reports called "transcripts" will be sent to churches to distribute to members participating in the Church Study Course. Each transcript will list courses and diplomas completed and will show progress toward diplomas currently being sought. The transcript will show which courses are needed to complete diploma requirements. A diploma will be issued automatically when the final requirement is met.

Complete details about the Church Study Course system, courses available, and diplomas offered may be found in a current copy of the *Church Study Course Catalog* and in the study course section of the *Church Materials Catalog*. Study course materials are available from Baptist Book Stores.

The Church Study Course system is simple enough to be

123

administered by volunteer workers with limited time. The system is universal so that credit earned in one church is recognized in all other Southern Baptist churches. Approximately 600,000 awards are earned by adults and youth each year.

The Church Study Course is promoted by the Sunday School Board, 127 Ninth Avenue, North, Nashville, Tennessee 37234; by Woman's Missionary Union, P. O. Box C-10, Birmingham, Alabama 35283-0010; by the Brotherhood Commission, 1548 Poplar Avenue, Memphis, Tennessee 38104; and by the respective departments of the state conventions affiliated with the Southern Baptist Convention.

How to Request Credit for This Course

This book is the text for course number 5161-15 in subject area: "Age Division and Special Group Characteristics." This course is designed for a minimum of five hours of group study. Credit for this course may be obtained in two ways:
1. Read the book and attend class sessions. (If you are absent from one or more sessions, complete the "Personal Learning Activities" for the material missed.)
2. Read the book and complete the "Personal Learning Activities." (Written work should be submitted to an appropriate church leader.)

A request for credit may be made on Form 725 "Church Study Course Enrollment/Credit Request" and sent to the Awards Office, Sunday School Board, 127 Ninth Avenue, North, Nashville, Tennessee 37234. The form on the following page may be used to request credit.

A record of your awards will be maintained by the Awards Office. Twice each year copies will be sent to churches for distribution to members.

CHURCH STUDY COURSE
ENROLLMENT/CREDIT REQUEST (FORM-725)

PERSONAL CSC NUMBER (If Known)

INSTRUCTIONS:
1. Please PRINT or TYPE.
2. COURSE CREDIT REQUEST—Requirements must be met. Use exact title.
3. ENROLLMENT IN DIPLOMA PLANS—Enter selected diploma title to enroll.
4. For additional information see the Church Study Course Catalog.
5. Duplicate additional forms as needed. Free forms are available from the Awards Office and State Conventions.

TYPE OF REQUEST: (Check all that apply)

☐ Course Credit
☐ Enrollment in Diploma Plan

☐ Address Change
☐ Name Change
☐ Church Change

REQUEST FOR

☐ Mr. ☐ Miss
☐ Mrs.

DATE OF BIRTH → | Month | Day | Year |

Name (First, MI, Last)

Street, Route, or P.O. Box

City, State, Zip Code

CHURCH

Church Name

Mailing Address

City, State, Zip Code

COURSE CREDIT REQUEST

Course No.	Use exact title
5161-15	1. **Ministering to Persons with Mental Retardation and Their Families**
Course No.	Use exact title
	2.
Course No.	Use exact title
	3.
Course No.	Use exact title
	4.
Course No.	Use exact title
	5.

ENROLLMENT IN DIPLOMA PLANS

If you have not previously indicated a diploma(s) you wish to earn, or you are beginning work on a new one(s), select and enter the diploma title from the current Church Study Course Catalog. Select one that relates to your leadership responsibility or interest. When all requirements have been met, the diploma will be automatically mailed to your church. No charge will be made for enrollment or diplomas.

Title of diploma	Age group or area
1.	
Title of diploma	Age group or area
2.	

Signature of Pastor, Teacher, or Study Leader	Date

MAIL THIS REQUEST TO

CHURCH STUDY COURSE AWARDS OFFICE
RESEARCH SERVICES DEPARTMENT
127 NINTH AVENUE, NORTH
NASHVILLE, TENNESSEE 37234

FORM-725 (Rev. 7-83)

89239